Get Real

Reality and Mystery

Michael Hickey

UNIVERSITY PRESS OF AMERICA, ® INC.
Lanham • Boulder • New York • Toronto • Plymouth, UK

Copyright © 2012 by
University Press of America,® Inc.
4501 Forbes Boulevard
Suite 200
Lanham, Maryland 20706
UPA Acquisitions Department (301) 459-3366

Estover Road
Plymouth PL6 7PY
United Kingdom

All rights reserved
Printed in the United States of America
British Library Cataloging in Publication Information Available

Library of Congress Control Number: 2011934941
ISBN: 978-0-7618-5659-7 (paperback : alk. paper)
eISBN: 978-0-7618-5660-3

∞™ The paper used in this publication meets the minimum
requirements of American National Standard for Information
Sciences—Permanence of Paper for Printed Library Materials,
ANSI Z39.48-1992

I dedicate this book to the Holy Spirit who has made the mystery of God a transcendent reality for me. I also dedicate this book to my parents, Ed and Mary, my wife Terri and my four children, Ed, Dave, Liz, Maryellen, and my grandaughter Katrina, all of whom I love and have loved me. They all have played the most significant roles in shaping my earthly reality.

Contents

Preface		vii
SECTION ONE: REALITY		**1**
1	Reality of Being	3
2	Roles of Truth and Belief	10
3	Reality of Life	14
4	Imagining the Real	18
5	The Final Earthly Reality	20
6	The Ultimate Reality	25
7	Self-Realizing	30
SECTION TWO: MYSTERY		**35**
8	Mystery?	37
9	Ancient Mystery Cults	40
10	Early Christianity: Another Mystery Cult	43
11	Sacramentality	47
12	Revelation: The Unveiling of God	50
13	Myth	55
14	Old Testament Mystery	59

15	New Testament Mystery	68
16	The Mystery of Suffering	75
17	Miracles Mystery	78
18	The Hidden Kingdom	82
19	Those Peculiar Parables	85
20	Mysticism	87
21	Two Types of Theological Mysteries	92
22	The Mystery of the Female	95
23	A Beginning and End Times Mystery	98

SECTION III: REALITY MEETS MYSTERY/ "THIS IS THAT" — **105**

24	Unity of Opposites	107
25	Personal and Universal	111
26	Matter and Spirit	115
27	Nature and Grace	118
28	Natural and Supernatural	121
29	Heaven and Earth	125
30	Time and Eternity	128
31	Knowing and Unknowing	131
32	Consciousness and Unconsciousness	135
33	Humanity and Divinity: The Cross +	138
34	Man the Reality and God the Mystery	142
35	God the Reality and Man the Mystery	145
36	Self-Transcending	148
37	Conclusion: God Mysteriously In Us and Us Really In God	151

Index — 153

Preface

"Get Real" was a slang term that became popular in the 1960s when I was a teenager growing up in East Boston. It implied that someone wasn't in touch with reality and had to change their way of thinking or living. The word "reality" is from the Latin *realis* which means "real existence."[1]

If you put on the television today, all you might find is one of the hundreds of so-called Reality TV shows. Back in the 60s, we had more mystery shows than reality TV shows. One of my favorites was *Alfred Hitchcock Presents*. I also liked many of the science fiction shows like *Twilight Zone* because they bordered on the mysterious. There weren't many Reality TV shows back then. Most of those that would have qualified were either game shows or talent shows, although one reality show I did like back then was *Candid Camera*.

Today Reality TV dominates the electronic entertainment media with unscripted, dramatic shows depicting "real life" or actual events. They use ordinary "real people" instead of actors or performers. Among the more popular shows are *Cops, America's Most Wanted, Survivor, American Idol, The Apprentice, The Bachelor, The Amazing Race, Fear Factor, Hell's Kitchen, Deadliest Catch, The Osbournes, Big Brother, Dancing With The Stars, Who Wants To Be A Millionaire, The Biggest Loser, So You Think You Can Dance*, and the list goes on.

Reality TV, in all its versions, represents from the producers' and broadcasters' standpoint, an attempt to respond to the changing economics of modern television programming. It is relatively cheap to produce, and it garners a niche audience in large enough numbers to sell the programs to potential advertisers. Ironically, it also offers the average "real" individual an unrealistic dream of potentially escaping from their day to day reality and transcending it. They imagine that they will ultimately flower into a greater individual and that their reality will be more appealing than what it had been previously. Being a Reality TV contestant can potentially make you a celebrity for the duration. You do have a very slim chance of continuing in the celebrity role afterwards. In reality, your odds are probably better for hitting the lottery.

Furthermore, I have found in watching some of these shows that, more often than not, they are illusions of reality because the "real persons" utilized as actors/performers are seemingly coached to act in certain ways by the directors, judges, or producers who really control the reality. Events, stories, and dialogue appear that they might be manipulated, creating not a real world environment, but a controlled or fabricated one.

None the less, Reality TV is a modern phenomenon; people watch it constantly, and that does indicate a high degree of the public's interest in some concept of reality. But enough about Reality TV, for it is not my intention with this book to get into any broad discussion of the subject, but to establish the fact that a large segment of the general public is interested in "reality." Suffice it to say, the factual evidence is established in that it is all over the small screen. What I would like to accomplish with this book is to move reality to a bigger screen, and I don't mean from the TV to the movie theater screen.

As for "mystery," there is no screen other than our own personal, societal, religious, environmental, or cultural screen. But, you would think that we are approaching an age where there will be the death of mystery, and we will have only reality. I think this is because the vast majority of the populace doesn't view reality in the context of mystery; they mistake reality and mystery for something other than what they really are. They imagine mystery to be something which is just obscure or ambiguous, which given enough time, will be solved by reason and logic and become reality. It's imagined to be more like an unsolved enigma. Mystery is only something which is not grasped now, but it eventually will be. That is not what mystery "is," but it is a lot easier to say what mystery "is not" than to say what mystery "is."

My hope is that this book, *GET REAL*, will give the reader a fresh understanding of both reality and mystery as seen from a theological and philosophical viewpoint. Ultimately, I would like to have the understanding move beyond the perceived duality and establish that mystery is truly the home of all reality.

NOTES

1. "Reality." Douglas Harper, ed., Online Etymology Dictionary. Found online at http://www.etymonline.com/index.php?search=reality&searchmode=none (Accessed 12/5/10).

Section One

REALITY

"Generally, by the time you are Real, most of your hair has been loved off, and your eyes drop out and you get loose in the joints and very shabby. But these things don't matter at all, because once you are Real you can't be ugly, except to people who don't understand." (The Velveteen Rabbit, A Children's Story by Margery Williams).

Chapter One

Reality of Being

REALITY

Reality is the quality or state of being real, authentic, and genuine. It has a basis in actual fact and truth. It includes everything that is, no matter whether observable or comprehensible, visible or invisible. Reality is certainly far more complex than what our immediate sense experience can tell us. The senses of seeing, hearing, tasting, smelling, and touching provide us with our immediate sense experience, but reality and the criteria for what is considered as "real" in our world is mediated by meaning.

The real is known to us through judgements and beliefs which give us meaning and our personal sense experiences of reality are simply not enough alone to tell us what is real. We need other people to be involved in understanding reality. Having other people relate what their reality is can be helpful in order to come to an understanding of it.

First, because appearances are deceiving there is no guarantee that what we are personally seeing, perceiving, or immediately experiencing through our senses is what is real. Intuition or a kind of sixth sense beyond our five senses does help us here, but is inadequate to convey the fuller meaning of what is real. Because reality is dynamic and "mediated by meaning," what occurs is that reality constantly changes as meaning changes over time.

Words can die a static death in time so reality, because it is dynamic, must of necessity transcend the words alone. Take the word "family," for example; on the one hand we are all convinced that a family is a reality and it exists. We speak about families, we think about families, we think we see them in reality, and each of us thinks of ourselves as part of some known family. Yet, none of us can really "touch" a family in reality or "see" a family in reality. A family is more than what we see or touch on the physical level through our sense experience. What a family "is," is a judgement and belief and is a reality that is constituted with meaning.

Because it is "mediated by meaning," the meaning can shift over time. For example, there used to exist only the nuclear family or traditional family; a father, a mother, and some children. Today in many minds, there exists the single parent family, extended family, communal family, church family, partnered family, work family, etc. Because the reality of "family" is constituted with meaning, the reality has changed as the meaning has changed over time. Reality can then only be dynamically understood over time through judgements and beliefs held in common.

In discussing reality, I should state at the outset, that what I am focusing on in this book is "reality of being." This is different from such things that are restricted categories of reality, such as mathematics, or hypothetical, and logical realities. These are spheres that can be affirmed rationally. "Reality of being" is affirmed by living life, spiritual experience, and consciousness which arises after reflection and contemplation on mystery. It leads one ultimately into the silence of wonder and love. In the dynamic state of love of God, our consciousness is different than our knowledge. To quote theologian, Bernard Lonergan, "Consciousness is just experience. Knowledge is a compound of experience, understanding, and judging. Because the dynamic state is conscious without being known, it is an experience of mystery."[1] Therefore, reality of being can be a conscious experience, though not fully realized or known.

Because reality is constituted with meaning and the meaning itself is continually changing over time, reality always has a future, unknown, and unrealized quality. In that reality has this future quality and the future is always unknown and unrealized for human beings, mystery can only be its true home.

REALITY OF BEING

Reality of being cannot be confined to a restricted category of reality because it is not univocal. The term does not have only one meaning and is not an unambiguous term. One finds that there is no clear and rational definition of the term, the understanding of which leads you to only one conclusion.

On a broad level, the private experiences, personal interactions, observations, formation, and development involved in the personal interpretation and perception of events shapes our individual reality. Here reality can be seen by one and only one individual. This form of reality might also be common to others as well, but at times could also be so unique to oneself as to be never experienced or agreed upon by anyone else. Much of the kind of experience which is deemed as "spiritual" occurs on this level of reality. Therefore, when we speak of "reality of being," we must often refer not to any one specific or individual reality but to many realities. In many ways, we each have our own ability to express what it means to us.

Ontology is the philosophical study of the nature and reality of being in general, as well as of the basic categories of being (such as existence) and their relations. It is traditionally listed as a part of the major branch of philosophy known as metaphysics. Aristotle is often considered as the first philosopher who broadly undertook a complete, definitive, and exhaustive study of metaphysics. Ontology inquires into being insomuch as it is being or in that it is being in reality. It asks the question stemming from an ancient Greek phrase put forth initially by Aristotle, *"To ti en einai?"* meaning "What does it really mean to be?"[2] And to which Shakespeare subsequently popularized in *Act III, Sc. 1* of the play *Hamlet* as "To be or not to be, that is the question."[3]

The Oxford English Dictionary of Current English, (as do most English dictionaries) renders a definition of "reality" as

1. the state of things as they actually exist, as opposed to an idealistic or notional idea of them.
2. a thing that is actually experienced or seen.
3. the quality of being lifelike.
4. the state or quality of having existence or substance.[4]

These dictionary definitions seem to render a static and not dynamic concept of reality. They seem to restrict any understanding of reality of being to be something synonymous with existence. They do not seem to consider either spirituality or make any assumption that there is a distinction and correlation between existence and essence in reality. Being, as "isness" is seemingly confined strictly to a discussion of existence. Being makes no provision for becoming. This is certainly not something which developed out of Aristotle's *Metaphysics*. For Aristotle, there was a world of difference between existence and essence.

We get our English word, "essence," from the Greek "ousia" (being) and later from the Latin word "esse" (to be) or (is). It can be translated to mean "the permanent act of being or the very nature of something as opposed to its existence."[5]

So, it is primarily from the ancient philosopher Aristotle that we get our modern thoughts about essence. He was a student of Plato. For Plato, "existence" ran a distant second to "essence" as a way of being. To see the real world was to see the ideal world and to see it as a system of essences. For

Plato, the idea or ideal was the real. What Plato called idea or ideal, Aristotle called essence, and its opposite, he referred to as matter. Matter is without shape or form or purpose. It is just "stuff;" pure potential, no actuality. Essence is what provides the shape or form or purpose to matter. Essence is "complete," but it has no substance, no solidity. Essence and matter need each other!

Christian, Jewish, and Islamic medieval philosophers made Aristotle's writings the groundwork of their commentaries in which they expanded and enriched Aristotle's thought in the light of Revelation. Averroes, Moses Maimonides, Thomas Aquinas, and Francisco Suárez were some of the more well known. The *Metaphysical Disputations*[6] of Suarez is one of the most thorough works on ontology in any language.

Beginning in the early Christian community, the gospel writer John will tell us about the reality of being in the opening words of his gospel: "He was in the beginning with God. All things came to be through him, and without him nothing came to be. (Jn 1:2–3)" and much later in the middle ages, Aquinas, in discussing reality of being would state in his *Summa*

> "One" does not add any reality to "being;" but is only a negation of division; for 'one' means undivided 'being.' This is the very reason why 'one' is the same as 'being.' Now every being is either simple or compound. But what is simple is undivided, both actually and potentially. Whereas what is compound, has not being whilst its parts are divided, but after they make up and compose it. Hence it is manifest that the being of anything consists in undivision; and hence it is that everything guards its unity as it guards its being."[7]

Aquinas maintained that essence and existence are in God and that all of the created order participates in the being of God. He would write, "Everything exists because it has being."[8] But only in God is essence and existence the same (ex. God is good; God is love). If one's essence in the created order is not their being, they still participate by existing in the reality of being itself. Therefore, every created reality participates in the reality of being of God, the Creator.

In the Thomistic tradition, modern theologians, such as Karl Rahner (who has been called a "transcendental Thomist) have referred to the reality of being in terms of what is called a "supernatural existential." Rahner discusses this supernatural existential first as "an ontological statement," then as "an appeal to reality," and a "realizing of the essence of grace in a radical way."[9] He sees the supernatural existential to be "a permanent modification of the human spirit which transforms its natural dynamism into an ontological drive to the God of grace and glory."[10]

So, it is essence which realizes ("makes real") matter. Essence spiritualizes matter. Therefore, any ontological discussion concerning reality of being is not complete unless at some point it comes around to discussing either essence or spirituality and not simply existence. Both what is actual and what is potential must be considered in determining what is "real" in the context of "being." If reality of being restricts itself to a static discussion only on the level of human existence as we know it, it will always be rational and incomplete knowledge at best. In the worst sense, it will never become a meaningful dialogue about either consciousness or reality.

Because "reality of being" must always take into account the act of "becoming," within human persons, its orientation is necessarily to the future, which for any human being is unrealized and shrouded in mystery.

In the present moment, because of our pride, we in our selfishness and egoism, may be inclining ourselves more to what is unreal than what is real. This unfortunately creates an illusion. We orient ourselves more and more to unreality and away from reality. The unfortunate thing is that we may never "realize" it. It is an unreality, however, to which we are more than happy to give ourselves completely. Reality can only change for us when we begin to realize the self-giving nature of God. Only in God can we begin to realize our true reality of being. For it is only in God, that we live and move and have our being. When someone is asked, or asks themselves, "Who are you?" this is primarily a questioning of their reality.

The person is capable of beholding their true self. "Know thyself," means to the person: Know thyself as being. Because the ego sets oneself apart from others and from God, the ego moves away from the reality of being and wallows in the illusion of being.

REAL, AUTHENTIC, GENUINE, ACTUAL

When something is real, it is said to be authentic. Its origin is genuine, accepted by, and supported by unquestioned evidence. The word "authentic" is from the Greek *authentikos* and the Latin *authenticus* meaning "original or primary." It is equivalent to *authentes* (aut + hentes) which translates as "doer." It has the same root as the word "author" which means "creator or originator." All of these translations have the same basic root and that is the Greek word *autos*, which translates into English as "self."[11]

When something is real it is also said to be genuine, which defines it as possessing the quality and character of origin. It proceeds from the original. "Genuine" is a word which comes into our language from the Latin *genuinus* meaning "natural." The root of the word is *genus*, which is the same word in both the Latin and the English, which defines someone or something as being of a certain kind or species in reality.[12]

When something is real, it is further said to be actual. It exists in act or in fact. It is to be involved in acting, action, or actuality. To act is to do in reality, and an actor is a doer in reality. Actuality and actualization pertain to actual existence in reality. When someone or something is actualized, they are then realized in action. Although the terms "real" and "actual" are often used synonymously and interchangeably, the dictionary does make one distinction between the two terms. "Real," particularly should apply to facts rooted in nature and "actual" to facts as they now are or have become. Implying that one may have had a different idea of them previously or the facts themselves may have been changed by circumstances. On the other hand, the dictionary goes on to state that "true" may be used of that which is in accord with the real or the actual (see *Random House Dictionary of the English language*).[13]

NOTES

1. Bernard Lonergan, Method in Theology, Lonergan Research Institute, ed., (Toronto, Canada: University of Toronto Press, 1990) p. 106.
2. Aristotle, Metaphysics, David Bostock, ed. (New York, New York: Oxford University Press, 1995) p. XI.
3. William Shakespeare, Hamlet, Act III, scene I, Shakespeare's Hamlet, Karl Elze, ed. (Berlin, Germany: Herausgegehen Pub., 1857) p. 45. Found online at Googlebooks .com http://books.google.com/books?id=Rps0AAAAMAAJ&pg=PA45&dq=to+be +or+not+to+be+that+is+the+question+shakespeare+hamlet&hl=en&ei=qRL9TO_ wHo-7ngf3lNjICg&sa=X&oi=book_result&ct=result&resnum=1&ved=0CCgQ6AE wAA#v=onepage&q=to%20be%20or%20not%20to%20be%20that%20is%20the%20 question%20shakespeare%20hamlet&f=false (Accessed12/5/10).
4. "Reality." Oxford English Dictionary, Edition II, Volume 1, John Simpson, Edmund Weiner, ed., (Oxford, England: Clarendon Press, 1993).
5. "Essence." Douglas Harper, ed., Online Etymology Dictionary. Found online at http://www.etymonline.com/index.php?search=essence&searchmode=none.
6. Fransisco Suarez,S.J., Metaphysical Disputations, Alfred Fredosso, ed., (New Haven, CT: Yale University Press, 1994).
7. Jn 1:2-3, New American Bible, St. Joseph Edition, Confraternity of Christian Doctrine, Board of Trustees/ National Conference of Catholic Bishops/United States Catholic Conference, Administrative and Editorial Committee/Board (New York, NY: Catholic Book Publishing Co., 1970). See also Thomas Aquinas, Summa Theologica, Q. 11, Ans. 1, From the New Advent Encyclopedia, found on the New Advent CD-ROM by Kevin Knight (Denver, CO: Advent International, 2009). See also the New Advent website at http://www.newadvent.org/summa/1011.htm#article1 (Accessed 12/5/10).

8. Thomas Aquinas, Summa Theologica, Q. 5, Articles 1–6, From the New Advent Encyclopedia, found on the New Advent CD-ROM by Kevin Knight (Denver, CO: Advent International, 2009). See also the New Advent website at http://www.newadvent.org/summa/1005.htm.

9. Karl Rahner, S.J., Foundations of Christian Faith, Mark Fischer, ed., (New York, New York: Crossroads Publishing, 1982) pp. 126–127.

10. Karl Rahner, S.J., A Rahner Reader, Gerald McCool, ed. (New York, NY: Seabury Press, 1975) p. 185.

11. "Authentic." Douglas Harper, ed., Online Etymology Dictionary. See Etymonline.com at http://www.etymonline.com/index.php?search=authentic&searchmode=none (Accessed 12/7/10).

12. "Genuine." Douglas Harper, ed., Online Etymology Dictionary. See Etymonline.com at http://www.etymonline.com/index.php?search=genuine&searchmode=none (Accessed 12/7/10).

13. "Actual." Douglas Harper, ed., Online Etymology Dictionary. See Etymonline.com at http://www.etymonline.com/index.php?search=actual&searchmode=none see also "Real." The Random House Dictionary of The English Language, Jess Stein and Laurence Urdang, ed. (New York, NY: Random House Publishing, 1966) p.1196.

Chapter Two

Roles of Truth and Belief

TRUTH: BEING IN ACCORD WITH REALITY

Truth is a judgement, proposition, or idea that is truthful because it is in accord with reality and is free from error, distortion, falsity, misrepresentation, and lies. To be erroneous, distorted, false, misrepresented, or a lie, is to be essentially unreal. The more we arrive at the discovery of truth in the world, the clearer our understanding of reality; the less truth, the greater the illusion of reality.

But, truth has no single definition upon which the majority of people agree. You only have to look at all the disagreements about what different people believe is true in reality to understand that. Various theories of truth continue to be debated. There are differing claims about what constitutes truth; how to define and identify truth; the roles that revealed and acquired knowledge play; and whether truth is subjective, relative, objective, or absolute. In one sense, every existing thing in reality is true in that it is the expression of an idea which exists in the mind of God.

In the ancient Hebrew world, truth (*emet, H.*) as described in the Old Testament, was expressed as part of a greater reality which incorporated not only truth, *(emet, H.)*, but judgement, (*mispat*, H.), justice, (*sedaqa*, H.), and steadfast love, (*hesed, H.*). Truth, to the Hebrew, also designated something faithful, firm, solid, real, and authentic.[1] In the Christian New Testament, Jesus tells us that the word he brings is truth, that he is himself the truth, the spirit will lead us to the truth, and that ultimately, the truth will make us free.[2]

Defining truth is one thing; to ask how we know that we have judged truly, quite another. To actually be able to define truth then, involves judgement and belief. We must first possess it and know that we possess it; i.e., must be able to distinguish it from error. We cannot define that which we cannot distinguish. The distinction of truth and error is, in the final analysis, intuitional, and it involves belief and a perception of reality. It is often with the appearance of things that our judgment is made rather than with their essential nature.

With regard to the intellect we use to discern truth, we must not allow irrelevant considerations to affect our perception of reality. We should avoid any rush to judgment and, as much as possible, get rid of bias, prejudice, and an overanxious will to believe something is the truth before we know it is true. Aristotle's definition of truth was "If a man says of what is that it is, or if he says of what is not that it is not, then he speaks the truth."[3] Aquinas believed that truth was "in conformity with truth in the Divine Mind of God."[4] When applied to ourselves, the habit of speaking the truth is considered virtuous and should be spoken, not only to be in accord with reality and free from error, distortion, falsity, misrepresentation, and lies. We should speak the truth in love because we know that, in reality, it also contributes to the building of our integrity and character.

Theoretically, since whatever is true is good and just, true judgments ought to result ultimately in good consequences and produce justice. It has to do with being honest, honorable, and accurate in our words and actions in reality. So, we should not tell a lie even to defend ourselves. We should never bias truth with prejudice or attempt to distort reality. Truthful people are sincere; they are in agreement with reality, to the best of their knowledge. They are truthful in word and deed. Therefore, when one is truthful, they are essentially "being in accord with reality."[5]

BELIEF: BEING IN ACCORD WITH TRUTH IN REALITY

If faith can be seen as personal knowledge of God, then belief is the formulation of the body of knowledge of God through communal faith. Belief is essentially an expression of faith. It can also be seen as an acceptance of truth without clear and convincing evidence or proofs which we personally verify. But, belief does help us to articulate the knowledge we have of God. In a progression; faith leads to theology (faith seeking understanding), and then theology leads to belief. But these are not static concepts. They are dynamic and as they impact upon each other, and interrelate, they can change. Faith, theology, and belief should always be in accord with the truth, and the truth should be in accord with reality. Paul would write to the Corinthians, "We too believe and therefore speak (2 Cor 4:13)." And then Augustine and many others after him would write, "I believe, therefore I understand."[6]

The truths of faith will always provide some degree of understanding and make sense to one who is a believer; to an unbeliever they will be utter nonsense. Because for those who believe, no proof is necessary; for those who do not believe, no proof will ever be enough. Belief then, can never prove the existence of God as a truth which is in accord with reality. It can only, through the inward movement and acceptance of grace, try to ground that belief in an understanding of the reality which is experienced as a transcendent reality.

Belief and truth most often involve others in reality. Although truth is always in accord with reality, the fact of the matter is that in the end, there are far more truths that we simply believe in life than we personally verify as truths. For example, we could never personally or critically assess all of the data upon which scientific proofs are made. We also live in a modern world where the flow of information from all parts of the world bombards us. A tsunami in the Indian ocean, an earthquake in Haiti, a plane crash in Pakistan; this and other information we receive every day is often accepted as truth without our individual verification of it as truth in reality.

The reality is that, we as human beings, who seek the truth, must often live simply by belief. In believing, we are often "trusting" the truth as acquired and confirmed by others as for the most part, there is no personal or individual verification of evidence. Then the first question for us really becomes . . . Without our personal verification, what truths are we believing are in accord with reality?

Therefore, if most of what we accept as reality every day can never be individually verified by us, then in the end, faith, belief, and truth become inner-realities. Although inner-realities are personal realities, they are not necessarily private realities. They are inner-realities held communally. Then the next question that remains for us is . . . Who and what do we believe as we attempt to understand ALL of what we consider as "reality?" In the final analysis, we are all simply believers. We don't have any other choice.

For example, the Bible is a record of faith, belief, truth, and reality as seen by others before us. But, faith-filled Christians believe that the expression of all of these is not simply a human construct or communication. It is also an expression of the self-communication of God, the transcendent reality, who inspired the human writers and reporters. The Bible, carries an authority as a recorded report of faith and belief, truth and reality that no other source can equal.

So, trusting the truth as examined, witnessed, and communicated by Matthew, Mark, Luke, John, Paul, and a host of martyrs and other Christians who have gone before us, is certainly preferential for us as Christians trying to understand reality. In the final analysis, for much of the world, it is no different than the way they entrust truth to countless unknown others each and every

Roles of Truth and Belief 13

day to assess what each of us calls "reality." To quote Teilhard de Chardin, "At the present time many believers, to avoid the anxieties that contact with reality might renew in them, allow a veil of conventional answers to cover the mysteries of life ."[7]

NOTES

1. "Truth," From Raymond E. Brown, S.S., Joseph A. Fitzmeyer, S.J., Roland E. Murphy, O. Carm., ed., Jerome Biblical Comm., (Englewood Cliffs, NJ: Prentice Hall Inc., 1968) Sects. 3:63; 6:20–24; 11:29; 16:14,54; 31:39; 57:18–22; 63:11: pp. 60, 106–107, 222, 269, 279, 353–355, 416, 518.

2. John 5:24; 14:6; 16:1–13; 8:32, New American Bible, St. Joseph Edition, Confraternity of Christian Doctrine, Board of Trustees/ National Conference of Catholic Bishops/United States Catholic Conference, Administrative and Editorial Committee/ Board (New York, NY: Catholic Book Publishing Co., 1970).

3. Aristotle, Nicomachaen Ethics, Book II, ch. 6, From Daniel C. Stevenson, ed., transl. W. D. Ross, Internet Classics Archives (Stilwell, KS:Digireads.com Publishing, 1994). See http://classics.mit.edu/Aristotle/nicomachaen.mb.txt (Accessed 12/8/10).

4. Thomas Aquinas, Summa Theologica, Question 16, Articles 1–8, Question 109, Articles 1–4, Found on the New Advent CD-ROM by Kevin Knight, New Advent Encyclopedia, (Denver, CO: Advent International, 2009). See New Advent at http://www.newadvent.org/summa/1016.htm#article1 and http://www.newadvent.org/summa/3109.htm#article1 (Accessed 12/8/10).

5. "Truth," Peter Mark Roget, from Christopher Orlando, Sylvester Mawson, ed., Roget's Thesaurus of the English Language in Dictionary Form, (Garden City, NY: Garden City Publications, 1940) p.522.

6. Augustine, The Works of Augustine, Vol X, Marcus Dods, ed., (Edinburgh, GB: T & T Clark and Co., 1873) p. 385 Found online at Googlebooks.com http://books.google.com/books?id=FP4XAAAAYAAJ&pg=PA385&dq=augustine+I+believe+therefore+I+understand&hl=en&ei=6Gz_TMCzHaKxnAfWw5izCw&sa=X&oi=book_result&ct=result&resnum=2&ved=0CCgQ6AEwAQ#v=onepage&q&f=false.

7. Pierre Teilhard de Chardin, Human Energy, The Spirit of the Earth, J. M. Cohen, ed., (New York, NY: Harvest Books, Harcourt Brace Jovanovich, 1962) p. 19.

Chapter Three

Reality of Life

REALITY AND CREATION

The term "creation" signifies both the action of God and the objective reality created. The Spirit and the Word of God are creative forces signifying action. As the objective reality, creation discloses the reality of God. In that sense, it is an echo or a mirror. Only God is uncreated reality. God, who is "Holy Mystery/Wholly Mystery," is a transcendent reality.[1]

Creation refers to the way in which the world and everything in the world has its origin, ground, life, and end in God. It embraces the whole reality of the world, not just the beginning, but the entire existence of the world, including the end of history and reality as we know it.

Creation is the original, ongoing, and eventually culminating act of God, by which reality is produced from nothingness. Creatures depend upon God for their life and existence. Everyone has a God question, which is a question of decision. The question in its ultimacy exists in the creature as either the lover who is seeking to love and know God more in reality or the unbeliever who is seeking to escape God as a reality. Without looking at creation through the lover's eyes, creation is too evil for a loving God to exist. Therefore, to the unbeliever, God is not real. In creation, there is always more reality to be seen and experienced. As God's creatures, we, as humans, can experience more and more, the fruit of creation's reality as we grow in love and knowledge.

Creation also shows the relationship between God and reality, and particularly between God and God's creatures. Creation discloses and will continue to disclose God. Creatures in creation can particularly manifest the divine presence and the divine reality. In the incarnation of Jesus, God is identified with a creature in reality in the humanity of Christ. God and the creature are uniquely one. The whole of the creative process culminates in the reality of the human and divine nature of Jesus Christ.

Man (*homo*) is a hominid. Human persons are creatures of God, made in God's image. Creation includes the process of "hominization" which is the progressive development of human life, through grace, to higher and higher levels of conscious realities. These realities include self-consciousness and self-realization. Creation is Christocentric, therefore, all creatures are in movement toward the reality of Christ-consciousness and unification in Christ. Love is God's (and ultimately creation's) dynamic and active agent. The human person is the real object of God's love. S/he is a partner in creation, and in that sense is a co-creator. One who loves becomes a "new creature in Christ (2 Cor 5:17)."[2]

In the Old Testament accounts of creation, the Hebrew word *bara* is translated as "create." It is never used except with Yahweh as its subject. It is the kind of created reality that only Yahweh is capable of creating both by works and by word. In the New Testament, John, the gospel writer will state, "In the beginning was The Word (Jn 1:1) . . ."

First, he is showing, that Jesus is truly the creative Word of God who already existed, in reality, at the beginning of time. Secondly, the term "Logos/ The Word," as a description of Jesus is combining God's dynamic, creative word (Genesis) and personified pre-existent wisdom present at creation (Proverbs) with the ultimate intelligibility of reality (Hellenistic Philosophy).[3]

The will of Yahweh and the incarnation of Jesus Christ gives the entire history of creation an intelligibility of reality. It defines creation, not only in its origin in reality, but will also define the entire historical process of creation until history and reality as we know it, ends.

Humanity, life, the earth, and the universe; all that we see and experience, has been created by God or one of God's creatures, by, through, and with the grace of God. God acts, produces, and sustains reality out of nothingness. All that is reality in God or that chooses to be apart from God depends upon God for its existence. Although, both creatures and the Creator exist, however, as has been stated, only in God is existence and essence the same. God IS love and God IS good. Where there is love and goodness, God exists, and the presence of God can be experienced and essentially realized by creatures.

As Christians, we await our own resurrection, made possible by the resurrection of Jesus Christ from the dead. This resurrection is to be brought out of mystery and into a present and future reality. As Paul writes, "All creation groans and is in labor (Rom 8:22)" as it is being and becoming unified in Christ, who is the alpha and omega, our beginning and end point. Just as creation evidences that God is the creator and the source of all reality, just so will our own resurrection evidence for us that God, in Christ, is the unifying end point of all reality. Hear the echo?

OPENNESS TO REALITY

Reality is also life on life's terms. Openness is characterized by receptivity to reality in the form of new ideas, suggestions, or experiences of life. To be open is to be inwardly available in one's orientation to what is real; to not be closed to transcendence. It fosters an attitude of trust, ready accessibility, and approachability; it also enables us to seek reality through openness to mystery. With the practice of this, we begin to develop habits which are free from bias, prejudice, and unreasoned judgement. These block out light and truth, and end up being the reality of the ignorant. When we are open, we can freely choose to remove any barriers to grace. We will be free from masks, reserve or pretense. We can then invite the abiding presence of God which enables and empowers us to become someone other than who we are; someone better than who we are.

Openness implies that there may be occasions where we become vulnerable; that we might let our guard down, but without vulnerability, we cannot appreciate another's reality. It also implies that we are open to correction or criticism of our current knowledge. In order to be open, we must create some space within ourselves to sacrifice our own personal reality for a transcendent reality. This requires not only further conversion in our orientation to reality, but also unlearning and relearning the lessons of life.

All reality has a mysterious character. The visible is embodied and mediated by the invisible. Openness can lead to a new way of seeing reality. To be open is to be aware that there is more going on and more to life than what we can see with our eyes or sense experience. It is also knowing that all reality is imbued with the hidden presence of God. In truth, we must be open to seeing God's view of reality and ultimately be willing to surrender our own.

Throughout the vastness of the universe, the dimensions of realty mingle in spirit and matter. This reality surrounds the totality of all of life's created things. As it begins to reveal itself to us it draws us into its presence and here we sense that we are mystically within the heart of reality and in rhythm with its beat of life. Because we shouldn't be open to anything and everything that we perceive as real, openness does require reflection, contemplation, discretion, and discernment; it must be guided by and grounded in God-given wisdom. Openness to reality is also never in conflict with sacred scripture.

The more open we are, the more we will be sensitive to the rights and needs of other people. When we are open within ourselves, we will also recognize our human limitations and incompleteness. We can then be receptive, candid, and transparent with others. We will sense that we are living life a new way. We are beginning to "GET REAL."

REALITY OF RESURRECTED LIFE

Jesus is risen to new life. Jesus' resurrection is a new reality which we enter into and receive the Spirit in order to participate in the life-giving mission of the risen Christ. Christians who believe this await the reality of our own resurrection from the dead to new life. Unlike the crucifixion, the resurrection cannot be called a historical reality as there were no eyewitnesses to it. What we have in the gospels are appearance stories and empty tomb stories that have historical implications on the realities and the lives of many others. The reality of the risen Lord transcends history and concerns life on the other side of death.

In the meantime, the Spirit of the living Jesus is present to us and within us, empowering us to live out the gospel in word and life. Theology and the scriptures cannot answer every question for us concerning the resurrection. But, belief that Jesus is risen is our guarantee and hope that we too will one day rise to new life and live forever with God. Jesus tells us in the gospels, "I am the resurrection and the life, they who believe in me will live even though they die and whoever lives and believes in me will never die (JN 11: 25–26)." And Paul will also tell us in 1 Cor 15:19, "If only for this life we have hope in Christ, we are to be pitied more than all people."[4]

NOTES

1. "Creation." Douglas Harper, ed., Online Etymology Dictionary. Found online at http://www.etymonline.com/index.php?search=creation&searchmode=none.

2. 2 Cor 5:17, New American Bible, St. Joseph Edition, Confraternity of Christian Doctrine, Board of Trustees/ National Conference of Catholic Bishops/United States Catholic Conference, Administrative and Editorial Committee/Board (New York, NY.: Catholic Book Publishing Co., 1970).

3. John 1: 1–18, New American Bible, St. Joseph Edition, Confraternity of Christian Doctrine, Board of Trustees/ National Conference of Catholic Bishops/United States Catholic Conference, Administrative and Editorial Committee/Board (New York, NY.: Catholic Book Publishing Co., 1970) p. 145 and pertinent footnotes to Gospel of John ch. 1:1–18.

4. Rom 8:22; JN 11: 25–26; 1 Cor 15:19, New American Bible, St. Joseph Edition, Confraternity of Christian Doctrine, Board of Trustees/ National Conference of Catholic Bishops/United States Catholic Conference, Administrative and Editorial Committee/Board (New York, NY.: Catholic Book Publishing Co., 1970).

Chapter Four

Imagining the Real

IMAGINATION

The word "imagination" comes from the Latin verb "imaginari" meaning "to picture oneself."[1] Imagination, in the context of reality, is the ability to form mental images of reality in the mind. It allows us to deal resourcefully with unusual problems or to better imagine a knowledge of ways we might potentially overcome the experiences of reality. It is when we imagine reality that the power to realize it can become available through God's grace.

Imagination, in a sense, is dreaming in the daytime. All the greatest achieved realities began simply as figments of someone's imagination. Imagination gives way to vision and gives one a special way of looking at real life and the real world around us. It also enables someone to see images of ethical and moral realities. Because Imagination is the seed of reality and not exactly the same as reality, it is oriented to the future. When in the present, it can become aligned with the virtue of hope.

Images can be used as tools to explain meaning. Contrasting good with evil, for example, has often been done imaginatively through the use of stories, proverbs, fables, parables, metaphors, allegories, myths, poems, etc. With these, images as word pictures, create associations with reality in the mind to illustrate, compare, and contrast. We need look no further than the nearest Bible to find many examples of all of these.

Forming mental images of potential reality in the mind is not a new idea. The idea of imagery dates back as far as ancient Greece. It was the philosopher Aristotle who developed it as the first comprehensive cognitive theory. His teacher, Plato, had described something called "phantasma," a Greek word describing reflections in pools or mirrors. Aristotle developed the word to then describe appearances or images of reality that were developed and reflected in the psyche. He compared these mental images to seeing an inner painting in the mind.[2]

In using imagination, we form a mental concept not actually present to our reality. Images light up our senses and they don't have to be strictly visual experiences. They can create a word-picture that enhances not only the sense of sight, but other senses, such as hearing, touch, taste and smell as well. These can be described as "seeing reality in the mind's eye," "hearing it in our head," "imagining the feel of something real," and others.

Imagination is based on the idea. The idea is the actuality of reality. It is only in the finiteness of the human person with limited faculties that the real and the idea are separated. Similarly, there are corresponding separations between actuality, potentiality, and reality. A lot of our thinking, and even our perception, has to do not only with what is presently in reality, but what potentially might be realized. Imagination can best be described in the oft-repeated words of Robert F. Kennedy, "There are those who look at things the way they are and ask, why?... I dream of things that never were and ask, why not?"[3]

God, The Transcendent Reality, is the Father of our imagination. But, the universe hides God as much as it discloses him. Our soul, formed in his image and likeness, can reveal and infer God only through the movement of God's grace shining and reflecting on our human intellect and the universe of our ideas. But, this will never be sufficient enough to allow us to see his person or the fullness of his being. God, the Holy Mystery, will always remain outside the limits of our humanity and the seemingly boundless horizon of our imagination.

NOTES

1. "Imagine." Douglas Harper, ed., Online Etymology Dictionary. Found online at http://www.etymonline.com/index.php?search=imagine&searchmode=none.

2. Plato, The Writings of Plato, The Sophist, Seth Bernadette, ed. (Chicago, IL: University of Chicago Press, 1986).

3. Robert F. Kennedy, Quotes by Robert F. Kennedy from Quotationsbook.com, Amit Kothari, ed., found online at Googlebooks.com at http://books.google.com/books?id=Yj6DhLkwf2kC&pg=PP2&dq=quotation+Robert+Kennedy++%E2%80%9CThere+are+those+who+look+at+things+the+way+they+are&hl=en&ei=knv_TLSPF4zMngeA7_D6CQ&sa=X&oi=book_result&ct=result&resnum=1&ved=0CCUQ6AEwAA#v=onepage&q&f=false(Accessed12/8/10).

Chapter Five

The Final Earthly Reality

DESTINY: TOWARD THE FINAL EARTHLY REALITY

The modern theologian, Reinhold Niebuhr has said, "The wisdom about our destiny is dependent upon a humble recognition of the limits of our knowledge and power."[1]

Destiny is both the process by which persons come to be who they are, and the end result of a human "becomings" journey toward final earthly being. Each of us is shaping the person we are choosing to be. We are destined to be someone and choosing, in freedom, who will be that final, irrevocable, and real self.

We are in the process of not only self-transcendence, but also self-realization. Reality is shaping us, while at the same time, we are shaping reality. Our destiny is being shaped, in part, by people and events outside our immediate sphere of influence. However, there are free choices we make following our interaction with any persons or events which further shapes our individual destiny. All of us are dealt a hand of cards that is our life. But, all of us then choose how to play those cards.

There is much in our culture that distracts us from reflection and contemplation concerning our ultimate destiny. Yet, because it concerns the continuation of our earthly life on into eternity, we should and must find the time to do this. Any anxiety as regards our destiny is probably blended with our anxiety over death and dying. But, if we believe that God is our origin, then we will probably believe that God is our ultimate destiny. There have been and will be offers of grace in journeying toward our destiny and either our acceptances or rejections of that grace. Quoting Jesuit theologian Karl Rahner, "Man is the mid-point suspended between the world and God, between time and eternity, and this boundary line is the point of his definition and his destiny."[2]

Destiny is different than fate. Fate implies that there is no freedom of choice; it is an outcome determined by an outside reality which impacts upon a person. Destiny, on the other hand, implies that the person is participating in achieving an outcome through the exercise of free-will.

God is always in control of our fate. With God, the future is eternally present and thus God already knows our fate. At this moment in time, we have something to say about our destiny through the exercise of our free-will. At the junction of where the omnipotence of God intersects with our free-will lies the providence of God. Without the providence of God, either God would not be omnipotent or we would not be fully free. Destiny and fate become more interchangeable as words only when they are used in the past tense.

In addition to our own individual destiny, there exists a destiny of the universe. Our individual destiny is distinct from that of Jesus Christ, but certainly not unrelated to it. The modern theologian, Teilhard de Chardin, saw God in all of reality. He believed that because reality is dynamic and not static, the whole of the cosmic order is moving toward a goal or end point. Teilhard termed this end point, "The Omega Point."[3]

He equated the Omega Point with Christ and believed that all of history is in dynamic movement toward Christ. This Omega Point will bring about the unification of mystery and reality. But, because Christ is already present in the world, his presence already imbues all of reality and all of mystery with a Christic dimension. The universe is really Christocentric, therefore, our destiny is already interwoven with the destiny of Christ. Pierre Teilhard de Chardin would write, "Now, a Christ who extended to only a part of the universe, a Christ who did not in some way assume the world in himself, would seem to me a Christ smaller than the Real."[4]

DEATH: THE FINAL EARTHLY REALITY

"Glory to you who safe have kept
And have refreshed me while I slept;
Grant Lord, when I from death shall wake,
I may of endless light partake."

The above poem is an anonymous morning prayer. It has been said before that "Everyone wants to go to heaven, but nobody wants to die." The dictionary defines death as "The end of life."[5] That definition probably works for those who do not believe in God; who could only see death as an end to life and something to be feared. But, for those who do believe in God, our hope is that in death, life is changed, but not ended. Either way, however, whether you are a believer or an unbeliever; if you are an earthly being, death is your final earthly reality and limiting horizon.

The world has become different from what it would have been as a reality if Christ had not died. By Jesus' death, his human reality became a determining feature of the entire universe. To the innermost reality of the entire universe there now belongs the life and death of Jesus Christ poured out. Jesus' living, dying, and rising has permeated the entire cosmos, made it Christocentric, and is now at the heart of all created reality.

The artist's rendering of death is always shown as a robed skeleton carrying a scythe. Just the thought of this Grim Reaper sends chills up most people's spines. Anyone reading my words has never experienced the reality of death. Surely, you've experienced the reality of other people's deaths, but certainly not your own; and most of us are less fearful about our own deaths than of facing the deaths of those we love. Our own death will be a once in a lifetime, unique experience for each of us. Jesuit theologian Karl Rahner has said, "Our death is a culmination of the unrepeatable onceness of our personal human existence. We can share our life with others, but not our death. The onceness of death implies also its finality."[6]

Because death is a personal and universal reality, we all share the experience in common. Yet, because it is the most individual of all our human experiences, it is something that many classic poets have penned numerous lines about. These would include such notable poets as Shakespeare, Dante, Milton, Byron, Wordsworth, Tennyson, and Longfellow, just to name a few.

Death exposes the superficiality and triviality of much that we count as important in our lives and to which we dedicate many personal resources and much of our energy. All poetic, romantic, and idealized versions of human life are brought low by the reality of human death. For, it is death which sets the framework of our human existence on this planet as it forces us to face the radical finitude of our earthly existence. Death is a reality that limits all of our horizons.

Most of us acknowledge that everyone must die, but usually we tend to treat the reality of our own death as something impersonal, and we tend to put it off someplace way out in some indefinite future. Only by coming to terms with the world we live in can we come to terms with any anxiety or fear that surrounds our own dying. In doing this we allay any fears that our human death will somehow lead to our "non-being" or being "un-real."

Death is a final horizon that closes off the indefinite future for us and although death relativizes all of our grand designs, it is our hope that love can defy death because death cannot annihilate it; love is expansive and never ends. Therefore, a good and healthy perspective concerning death is to believe that if we die we will be with the God of mystery and meanwhile, while we live and love, God is with us in our reality. What follows is a poem I wrote while reflecting on love and my own death and dying.

HORIZONS

by Michael Hickey

Remote rim of
Defining distance;
Limiting level;
Boundary and
Baseline border;
Yet, immanent eyereach,
Visible field of view, and
Seeable scope as well;
Depending upon my
Participating position and
Perceptual parallax.
Junction of sea and sky,
Where heaven exits earth,
While earth hugs heaven;
It is you who say to me:
"This far and no farther—
That is all there is."
But within, the
Third eye of faith
Sees signs of a
Shifting spectrum;
Where hope hints
That love's limit
Is always lifting
It is there that,
Revelation recedes,
Exceeding reason's reach;
Until beyond beckons beyond
My alluring illusion of
Visible invisibility and
Unrealized reality;
Providing new questions of,
Unfinalized finality?

NOTES

1. Reinhold Niebuhr, Reinhold Niebuhr: His Theology in the 1980's, Robert McAfee Brown, ed. (Chicago, IL: Christian Century Press, 1986) Found online at Religiononline.com at http://www.religion-online.org/showarticle.asp?title=989.
2. Karl Rahner, Spirit in the World, (New York, NY: Herder and Herder/Crossroads Publishing, 1968) p.407.
3. "Omega Point." Pierre Teilhard de Chardin, The Phenomenon of Man, Bernard Wall, ed.(New York, NY: Harper and Row Publishing, 1959) pp. 57, 257–264, 268–272, 288, 291–298, 307–309.
4. Pierre Teilhard de Chardin, The Heart of Matter, Ren Hague, ed. (Boston, MA: Houghton Mifflin Harcourt, 1980) p. 201.
5. "Death." Merriam-Webster Dictionary, Henry B. Woolff, ed. (Springfield, MA: G & C. Merriam Co., 1974) p. 291.
6. Karl Rahner, The Practice of Faith, Karl Lehmann and Albert Raffelt, ed., (New York, NY: Crossroads Publishing, 1984) pp. 295–296.

Chapter Six

The Ultimate Reality

LOVE

The human person has a dynamism within which orients them toward an absolute being who is a transcendent reality. Love is a keyword for this mysterious dynamism in which the true and whole man is drawn away from his or her own reality and into the incomprehensible mystery we call "God." Christ's love is divine love *(hesed, H.; agape, Gk)*. It is God's love shared with humanity. It is unconditional, infinite, self-giving, and has the welfare of the other at heart. Only Christ has fully and perfectly "realized" this love on earth, but it is his mark in any Christian who is self-realizing in the Holy Spirit.[1]

Love is the essence of being-real, and it is the ultimate reality of being. In that it is a spiritual reality, it is dynamic *(dynamis Gk)*. Because it is dynamic, it is constantly in movement and can only be "realizing" when we do love and when we are loved. Love must be spiritually experienced, otherwise it cannot be known. Therefore, love, as a reality, has primacy to any knowledge.[2]

Through the acceptance of grace within, loving another begins with loving ourselves holistically. It is impossible to love another person without loving ourselves. This is implied, both in Old Testament law (Lv 19:18) and in Christ's words in all three Synoptic Gospels concerning loving our neighbor as ourselves (Mt 19:19; Mk 12:31; Lk 10:27). It is a point which the Apostle Paul confirms in his Letters (Rom 13:9; Gal 5:14)[3] and Aquinas later takes up in his *Summa* (Sum. Q. 25) not only referencing scripture, but also by quoting the philosopher Aristotle (Eth. IX:4,8). It is in coming to greater self-realization and growing understanding of the meaning of the word "self" that one comes to realize the importance of loving our "self" in the love dynamic.[4]

As the ultimate spiritual reality, love alone has the potential to unite human beings in such a way as to complete them and bring them to perfection. But, only in God is essence and existence the same. God's essence and existence is perfectly realized love. Therefore, if our essence as a human being is not perfect love, as is the case with God, then it can only be "change" as we orient ourselves to a loving God by loving others and being loved. The more we become "lovers," the more love becomes realized in our lives and other's lives as well.

Love loses its energy and spiritual power if it remains anonymous. All love is self-surrender. We cannot really love without loving another person and losing ourselves in that person(s). Therefore, love is the most personal of all realities. Because it is the most personal reality, that would make it the most universal as well. Love has a universal dynamism and dimension. This is not to say that we, personally, have enough loving potential for all of humanity. Only, that even loving the one or loving the few has both personal and universal consequences. Conversely, when the universe assumes a face, heart, and personality for us, then it becomes a most personal reality.

If we have had the personal experience of loving someone and being loved, that would indicate that love must have a source. If love has a source, where does it end? And if our own birth was not the source of love, can our own death be its end point? If love is the ultimate spiritual reality of being, then death can only bring change and transformation to our having loved; it cannot bring finality. Death may well be the final earthly reality, but love is the ultimate reality that will transcend dying.

Love will defy death because it is expansive and never ends (1 Cor 13:13).[5] Because of the love that is within us, our own death cannot lead to "un-love," or "un-being," or "un-reality." Our death can only lead back to the source of love which is God, Holy Mystery, or Transcendent Reality. All three of these terms mean the same Supreme Being.

God lives as the mystery of love within persons. Grace unites us to Christ and to one another in dynamic and active love. The dynamic movement of the Spirit gives us the grace to love ourselves, love God, and to love others. It insures not only the natural, but also the supernatural quality of that love. Love is the self-communication of the Spirit of God. The Spirit of God within us, through grace, makes possible the acceptance of the loving presence of God in Christ.

Love is also a longing for union, so all love ultimately leads to union. You can kill the flesh, but you cannot kill the spirit. As Paul writes, "Nothing can separate us from the love of God in Christ Jesus, our Lord (Rom 8:38)."[6]

If we love and are loved, then the essence of God which is God's Spirit is within us, and it is that same essence that is God's and that is love. This is the case even if we have loved imperfectly. Again, to be clear, this is not implying that "we are love." But, because God IS love, is within us in love, is totally other, and a transcendent reality; at our death, the "I" and the "Thou" will be transformed into a "We." There will be union and love will be as "realized" for us as it is for God.

If we, as Christians, live in faith, hope, and love, then we have entered new life and become "new creatures in Christ (2 Cor 5:17; Eph 4:24)" For creatures who have faith in God, at their last breath, their faith will become wisdom (realized experience) as faith moves from an unseen to a seen reality. For creatures who have hope in God, at their last breath, their hope will become wisdom (realized experience) as hope moves from being an unrealized to a "realized-reality." So, when faith yields to sight and hope yields to possession, for creatures who love God, in the end, at their last breath, there will only be love. Love is all there is, and ultimately, love is all there will be.[7] We will be realized in God and experience in love what it is like to ultimately and actually "GET REAL."

PURE LOVE

by Michael Hickey

Pure love penetrates the soul
Dissolving egos and fears
Perfection, its ultimate goal
Appearance to reality nears
Invisible and visible marries
Heaven and earth celebrate
Divisible no longer carries
Providence hath unified fate
Abolishing worldly strife
Creating soul's true heart
Releasing mystery of life
Cleansing earth; being apart
Pure Love, child newborn
Radiating beyond a taint
Gabriel blows his horn
Heralding one more saint.

GOD IN REALITY

As the scripture states so simply and beautifully, "God is love" (1 Jn 4: 8, 16).[8] But, it is the reality of that definition which always seems to elude us.

Webster's dictionary first defines the word "God" as "the supreme or ultimate reality;" then goes on to elaborate with several further embellishments to the simple definition of the word.[9] A word has a reality all of its own. It reveals its own essence if we move away from the word and begin to approach what it signifies or represents for us.

Using the mere word, "God" says nothing about what is meant by the one who uses the word. Nor does it point to any reality outside of the mere word. It reflects what it signifies, "The Nameless One." But, the word, "God," is not just any word. It belongs to our language in a special way, in that it is a reality in itself. We may be or may not be conscious of this reality, but the reality is always conscious of us, particularly in our questions.

In Jesus Christ, God is self-communicated and assumed a human nature, in history, as God's own reality. Therefore, God? The question, is intertwined with the questions, "Who is Jesus?" 'What is a human being?" or, "Who am I?"

Socrates said long ago, "Wisdom begins in wonder."[10] God is mankind's attempt to discuss or explain all the experiences of wonder. The word "God" questions all the words in the whole of language in which reality presents itself to us. It essentially asks, "what is reality?" God is not one reality among others. God IS other and is the ground of all reality. God is Transcendent Reality. Therefore, the word "God" will inevitably open up less to an understanding of the reality of The Being who is God, and more to an unfathomable and ineffable mystery which involves us.

It is this mystery which is not only the transcendent ground of all reality; It IS primordial reality which comprises everything and supports everything. God is reality and being itself. Every created reality participates in the being of God. To know that God is ultimate reality is one thing; to identify God's presence in reality, quite another. If we are actively pursuing an understanding of God, we are pursuing a transcendent reality which essentially is a mystery. We ultimately will find ourselves in the grasp of that mystery on which we were trying to "get a grip." The meaning and very understanding of the words "love," "God," "self," "being," and "reality" begin to be transformed. We eventually will realize in our self-realizing that we are losing ourself in God.

NOTES

1. "Love." Jerome Biblical Commentary, Raymond E. Brown, S.S., Joseph Fitzmeyer, S.J., Roland Murphy, O. Carm., ed., (Englewood Cliffs, NJ: Prentice Hall Publishing, 1968) Sec. 30:4,24; 42:73; 48:21; 52:20; 53:121,124; 62:25; 63:71, 142; 79:38,88.

2. "Augustinianism." Karl Rahner, S.J., Encyclopedia of Theology, The Concise Sacramentum Mundi, Karl Rahner, ed., (New York, NY: Seabury Press, 1975) pp. 58–60.

3. LV 19:18; MT 19:19; MK 12:31; LK 10:27; Rom 13:9; Gal 5:14, New American Bible, St. Joseph Edition, Confraternity of Christian Doctrine, Board of Trustees/National Conference of Catholic Bishops/United States Catholic Conference, Administrative and Editorial Committee/Board (New York, NY: Catholic Book Publishing Co., 1970).

4. Thomas Aquinas, Summa Theologica, Q. 25, Art. 1–12, From the New Advent Encyclopedia, found on the New Advent CD-ROM by Kevin Knight (Denver, CO: Advent International, 2009). See also the New Advent website athttp://www.newadvent.org/summa/3025.htm#article1.

5. 1 Cor 13:13, New American Bible, St. Joseph Edition, Confraternity of Christian Doctrine, Board of Trustees/National Conference of Catholic Bishops/United States Catholic Conference, Administrative and Editorial Committee/Board (New York, NY: Catholic Book Publishing Co., 1970).

6. Rom 8:38, New American Bible, St. Joseph Edition, Confraternity of Christian Doctrine, Board of Trustees/ National Conference of Catholic Bishops/United States Catholic Conference, Administrative and Editorial Committee/Board (New York, NY: Catholic Book Publishing Co., 1970).

7. 1 Cor 13:13; 2 Cor 5:17; Eph 4:24, New American Bible, St. Joseph Edition, Confraternity of Christian Doctrine, Board of Trustees/National Conference of Catholic Bishops/United States Catholic Conference, Administrative and Editorial Committee/Board (New York, NY: Catholic Book Publishing Co., 1970).

8. 1 Jn 4: 8, 16, New American Bible, St. Joseph Edition, Confraternity of Christian Doctrine, Board of Trustees/ National Conference of Catholic Bishops/United States Catholic Conference, Administrative and Editorial Committee/Board (New York, NY: Catholic Book Publishing Co., 1970).

9. "God." Merriam-Webster Dictionary, Henry B. Woolff, ed. (Springfield, MA: G & C. Merriam Co., 1974) p. 493.

10. Socrates, Dialogues of Plato, Civilization's Quotations, Richard Alan Kreiger, ed., (New York, NY: Algora Publishing, 2002) p. 86.

Chapter Seven

Self-Realizing

A REALIZING OF SELF

All of the energy in the reality of life is always dynamically moving. Self-realizing is the realizing of oneself in the dynamism of life. It is the transition from potentiality to reality. We are directed and oriented transcendentally beyond our self and toward reality, which because it is transcendent, will always surpass us and be mystery. I prefer the term "self-realizing" to "self-realization" because it represents the more active and dynamic process taking place now in time, space, or history.

For the Christian, we must first believe in faith that God in Christ is present within us as the principle and power of our self-realizing. It cannot occur apart from the movement and acceptance of grace and an orientation to Christ as the end point of history and reality as we know it ("The Omega Point").[1] You cannot separate the realizing from the Realizer or the one being realized.

Self-realizing is not something which can be directly equated with any kind of intellectual knowledge and it is not the result of any process of rational thought. Because it has to do with "reality of being," it is more so an experience of spiritual awareness and consciousness that is experienced as being realized apart from just intellectually knowing it. It is consciousness without knowledge. It can only be put into language following the experiences of self-realizing.

The process occurs after a period of self-surrender as one experiences the losing of oneself in God as a transcendent reality. It is interwoven with the process of self-transcending. We become more conscious of God's love for us and this increases our love for God and other persons. We begin to realize and actualize all of our potentialities and the trueself begins to emerge in Christ.

Because it is a spiritual experience, it manifests itself in the fruit of the Spirit in producing more love, joy, peace, patience, kindness, gentleness, faithfulness, humility, and self-control (Gal 5:22)[2] in real life; not only in our own life, but also in the lives of those around us. Reality is being transformed from within not as our action; but only by our acceptance of the grace.

Self-realizing brings the spiritual awareness that the totality of oneself is inextricably linked with Christ to God as a transcendent and ultimate reality. In the end, God really gives Godself to a Oneself. God is the reality into which all realities in time, space, and history are converging.

One freely decides to accept the realizing of oneself in Christ in responsibility and in freedom. Because freedom implies that there are and will be choices, self-realizing can also become self-refusing and ultimately self-refusal (Jesuit theologin, Karl Rahner, equates this with sin).[3] What surrounds the choices leading up to self-realization or self-refusal is the individual capacity to freely accept the grace of God's unconditional love and the reality of being in Christ. It is truly interiorizing and realizing Christ's words in the Gospels, "to love God with all your heart, with all your being, with all your strength, with all your mind, and your neighbor as yourself. (Lk 10:27; Mk 12:30)."[4]

Self-realizing relates us to God in the same way as a droplet of water relates to the ocean. This is not to say that the self realizes that the self is God, but rather that the self realizes that the self has the same "beingness" or "isness" as God or that the self is "being-realized" in God.

So, with self-realizing comes not only wonder and love, but the experience of fear and trembling as well. One of the roles of the Holy Spirit is to be the comforter, paraclete, or advocate (*L. ad-vocatus; Jn 14:16)*.[5] So, we can take comfort in the fact that the Holy Spirit lives as the presence of God in us. But, God is other and the Holy Spirit is also uncreated grace; the very self-communication of God. This means that, as creatures, our humanity is really graced nature and is essentially being realized in God. We are not essentially realizing God in us.

What this implies is that there is no point in the process of self-realizing where we ever really or actually become God. God remains a transcendent reality whose being will always be wholly other and Holy Mystery.

GET REAL

by Michael Hickey

Roses are red, violets are blue;
All reality is constituted by meaning;
Then real is not what I judge as true,
Nor experiences on which I'm leaning.

Some roses are pink and yellow
I've experienced white as well,
But, black was seen by a fellow,
Who rose after experiencing hell.

Life is short, but it's also wide,
Meaning, creates the larger world,
See, hear, taste, smell, touch inside,
Then outer complexities get hurled.

Answers to questions begin differing,
Black and white develops more gray,
Judgements; beliefs thus inferring,
There's more to experience today.

Appearances; mysteriously deceiving;
Always more than experience going on,
What I am personally perceiving,
Is graced in meaning and mediation.

Universal is more than my mind,
Reality changes; meaning surprises;
Personal is mediated in humankind
Collectively dreaming; consciousness rises.

Reality is not just self-evidenced,
Nor contained in any thought or idea,
It's reality that mystery has fenced,
As love conquers death, sin, and fear.

If reality, the unfolding of mystery,
Is shaped by One other than me,
Then it's partly transcendent of history,
Including those outside my reality.

Reality includes visible and invisible,
And is beyond the control of my senses,
Only through faith is it possible,
To trust more than just my experiences.

Mystery remains the well-hidden reality,
I can't know how much I don't know;
The supernatural appears in sacramentality,
That only signs and symbols can show.

Reality and mystery are sacramental;
My world and my universe included,
Thus communion becomes life essential,
Graced experience; not being self-deluded.

NOTES

1. Pierre Teilhard de Chardin, The Phenomenon of Man, Bernard Wall, ed.(New York, NY: Harper and Row Publishing, 1959) pp. 57, 257–264, 268–272, 288, 291–298, 307–309.

2. Gal 5:22, New American Bible, St. Joseph Edition, Confraternity of Christian Doctrine, Board of Trustees/ National Conference of Catholic Bishops/United States Catholic Conference, Administrative and Editorial Committee/Board (New York, NY: Catholic Book Publishing Co., 1970).

3. "Christianity." Karl Rahner, S.J., Encyclopedia of Theology, The Concise Sacramentum Mundi, Karl Rahner, ed., (New York, NY: Seabury Press, 1975) p. 198.

4. Lk 10:27; Mk 12:30, New American Bible, St. Joseph Edition, Confraternity of Christian Doctrine, Board of Trustees/ National Conference of Catholic Bishops/ United States Catholic Conference, Administrative and Editorial Committee/Board (New York, NY: Catholic Book Publishing Co., 1970).

5. John 14:16, New American Bible, St. Joseph Edition, Confraternity of Christian Doctrine, Board of Trustees/ National Conference of Catholic Bishops/United States Catholic Conference, Administrative and Editorial Committee/Board (New York, NY: Catholic Book Publishing Co., 1970).

Section Two

MYSTERY

Chapter Eight

Mystery?

MYSTERY?

The word *mystery* came into our language from the Greek *mysterion*, meaning "to shut or hide." This term signifies, in general, that which is unknowable, or valuable knowledge that is kept hidden or secret. The word appears several times in the Bible, as does another Greek word *apocalypsis* which is translated as "unveiling" or more literally "lifting the veil" or "revelation." The Greek word *mysterion* is rooted in other Greek words such as *mystos* which means "keeping silence" and *myein* which means "closed lips."[1]

Tracing the word *mysterion* and its usage in the Greek language, we find that the word was originally used to signify the place where religious ceremonies or rites took place. And more specifically, it was the place which was reserved for those acolytes who were being initiated into the mystery. The New Testament Synoptic Gospel writers as well as the Apostle Paul, in his letters, would later apply the word *mysterion* in different ways. They would apply the word in the sense of a Divine Plan of God, or when speaking about Divine Revelation which had heretofore been secret, but now revealed through Jesus Christ, having the salvation of mankind as its object.[2]

When mystery is now used in a theological sense, it implies that it is "a religious or a supernatural truth that man can only know through Divine Revelation."[3] At the heart of all mystery is "the secret," i.e. that which is or has been hidden knowledge. The secret is always "confidential" which is a word that came into our language from the Latin *con-fides* which implies that the secret should be shared only "with faith" or "with trust" in those who are about to receive it.[4]

A mystery is different from a puzzle, riddle, enigma, or conundrum in that these pose problems to the mind which are difficult, obscure, or ambiguous.

Potentially, these can be solved through reason, logic, and human understanding alone. To the modern mind, mystery often implies something more compatible to these. It represents little more than the unexplored and not-yet-understood aspects of reality. It becomes only a series of unanswered questions that reason and logic will eventually solve, but that is not the true understanding of mystery. This is also the principle reason why for many people there is no sense of mystery and it often seems to be absent from their lives today.

On the other hand, the use of the word *mystery* should never be applied to mean revealed truth which is totally incomprehensible to human intelligence or reason. If it is truth beyond reason, it remains unrevealed or veiled. The Trinity, for example, is different. It is a revealed truth, but it is also an Absolute Truth and Absolute Mystery, which moreover implies that even though it is revealed, we cannot fully grasp it or comprehend it with our finite minds.

Acknowledgment of the presence of mystery does not equate to capitulation to meaninglessness. We, of course, do not have full meaning, but neither do we have total mystery.

Much of the reality which is contained in mystery appears to us as out there on the horizon. But, as soon as we begin moving closer to the horizon, it moves further away from us and another horizon opens up for us. Beyond the reality we see and experience is mystery, and beyond any mystery revealed lies both more unknown reality and more unrevealed mystery.

The beginning point for any encounter with mystery is the grace of God creating a question within us. To have a question is to first of all go on a quest, to search or inquire. If God becomes a question for us and not a completely known and definitive reality, therein begins a search for God. God, for us, should be known and unknown, at once, reality and mystery.

Unless it is a rhetorical question, a question mark at the end of any sentence indicates what is unknown or unknowable, what essentially is mystery within our conscious reality. It is outside of our known or even perhaps knowable reality. Questions should not always simply lead to answers; they sometimes should lead to deeper and more profound questions.

Our questions will often lead us into the silence of reflection and contemplation. The God of mystery most often speaks out of silence. We will find that sometimes when we get to our center it is there that we frequently encounter the God of mystery. Most of the time we will be the one asking the questions, but every now and then, we will be the one being questioned. For while we have been looking for the God of mystery, the God of mystery has been looking for us in our reality.

NOTES

1. "Mystery." Douglas Harper, ed., Online Etymology Dictionary. Found online at http://www.etymonline.com/index.php?search=mystery&searchmode=none.
2. "Mystery." Jerome Biblical Commentary, Raymond E. Brown, S.S., Joseph Fitzmeyer, S.J., Roland Murphy, O. Carm., ed., (Englewood Cliffs, NJ: Prentice Hall Publishing, 1968) Sec.53:9, 140; 57:21–22; 55:21; 79:14, 20, 34, 153; 48:33; 51:18; 79:11, 32–34; 56:6, 14–15, 19, 38; 41:40–41.
3. "Mystery." " Karl Rahner, S.J., Encyclopedia of Theology, The Concise Sacramentum Mundi, Karl Rahner, ed., (New York, NY: Seabury Press, 1975) pp. 1000–1004.
4. "Confidence." Douglas Harper, ed., Online Etymology Dictionary. Found online at http://www.etymonline.com/index.php?search=confidence&searchmode=none.

Chapter Nine

Ancient Mystery Cults

NOT MYSTERY RELIGIONS

Many of the so-called "Mystery Religions" of antiquity were not religions at all, but "Mystery Cults" because all religious functions were closed to the uninitiated or non-inducted. The inner-workings of the cult were kept secret from the general public. In fact, those who were initiates were called *mystes* from the same root meaning of the word *mysterion*. In the mystery cults those of higher rank gradually revealed the mysteries of the cult to acolytes of lower rank.

Our knowledge of mystery, in this sense, began in pagan antiquity. Mystery cults were prevalent around the Mediterranean during the time of the development of the early Christian community in the late Hellenistic Age (100 BC-300AD).[1] The mystery cult of the Egyptian goddess, Isis, for example, which is said to date back to 2500 BC was described in the early writings of the Greek scholar, Plutarch. Isis was called "the mother of the gods." Her worship and the mystery that surrounded the rites of initiation spread throughout the Greco-Roman world.

Osiris, the husband of Isis, was said to be murdered by his brother, Set. Isis needed to resurrect Osiris from the realm of the dead for the purpose of having the child Horus with him. Supposedly, it was necessary for Isis to learn magic to do this. Isis tricked Ra *(i.e. Amun-Ra/Atum-Ra)* into telling her his "secret name," by causing a snake to bite him, for which only Isis had the cure. The names of deities were shrouded in mystery and not divulged to any but the religious leaders. Knowing the secret name of the deity enabled one to have the mysterious power of the deity. Mystery and magic were central to the entire myth of the ensuing Cult of Isis, more than any other Egyptian deity.[2]

The word "mystery" was also used to designate certain esoteric doctrines such as Pythagoreanism, which were mystical thoughts, beliefs, and rites held by Pythagoras and his followers who were influenced by mathematics. Many of these mysteries included the transmigration of the soul and the elevation of man to be in unity with the gods. They were an inspiration for the future *Dialogues* of the philosopher, Plato, and subsequently his followers, such as Aristotle. One can see these influences particularly in the writing of Aristotle's *Metaphysics* and *Ethics*.

There were also certain ceremonies that were performed in private or whose meaning was known only to the initiated, for example, the Dionysian and Eleusinian rites. In Greek Mythology, the god Zeus had intercourse with a mortal woman, Semele, and fathered Dionysus, the god of wine and religious ecstasy. This mystery cult is believed to have come to Greece from Thrace. The Dionysian Mysteries were rituals which utilized trance-inducing techniques, such as either intoxicants or dance and music to remove inhibitions. In this mystery cult, there was an emphasis on the transcendental and the mystical. Dionysus was believed to alter his nature to become a resurrected god. The cult also contained secret knowledge about the mystery of an afterlife.

The Eleusinian rites were religious ceremonies held at Eleusis, a city near Athens in ancient Greece. They were mysteries celebrated every year, beginning around 1600 BC. These mysteries were an outgrowth of the worship devoted to gods and goddesses, particularly Demeter, the goddess of fertility and agriculture and her daughter Persephone, fathered by Zeus. Persephone became the goddess of death and the underworld. The mysteries were also initiation rites which included unity with the gods and the promise and knowledge of an afterlife. The centrality of the mystery was the elevation of man above the realm of humanity and into the realm of the divine. There were a few other minor mystery cults such as the Orphic mysteries and the Mithraic mysteries. These were believed to be evolutionary outgrowths of the Eleusinian rites.

Many of the Gentiles coming into the early Christian community were very often converts from the various mystery cults. They probably would have tended to bring in some features with them from their former worship in the various mystery cults.[3]

NOTES

1. Jerome Biblical Commentary, Raymond E. Brown, S.S., Joseph Fitzmeyer, S.J., Roland Murphy, O. Carm., ed., (Englewood Cliffs, NJ: Prentice Hall Publishing, 1968) Sec 41:40–41.

2. Plutarch, The Complete Writings of Plutarch, R. W. Emerson, ed. (New York, NY: Colonial Co. 1906) Found online at http://books.google.com/books?id=ZJ5bGwAACAAJ&dq=the+complete+writings+of+Plutarch+colonial&hl=en&ei=I_L_TITfF9GknQfe-dXlDQ&sa=X&oi=book_result&ct=result&resnum=1&ved=0CCYQ6AEwAA.

3. Jerome Biblical Commentary, Raymond E. Brown, S.S., Joseph Fitzmeyer, S.J., Roland Murphy, O. Carm., ed., (Englewood Cliffs, NJ: Prentice Hall Publishing, 1968) Sec. 41:40–41 see also Encyclopedia of Ancient Greece, Nigel G. Wilson, ed., (New York, NY: Routledge Publishing/ Taylor and Francis Group, 2005).

Chapter Ten

Early Christianity: Another Mystery Cult

THE DISCIPLINE OF THE SECRET

The early Christian community has occasionally been referred to as another one of the "Mystery Cults" by some due to the fact that worship was in secret and meetings were shrouded in mystery. This is not accurate, of course, because the term should not be so loosely applied to religious groups who are forced to worship secretly because of the prevailing existence of hostile persecution.

Furthermore, as the Apostle Paul would point out in several of his letters to the fledgling Christian churches, the secret plan of God, this *mysterion*, was not meant for a privileged few who were initiates, but for the entire world.[1]

On the other hand, the *Discipline Of The Secret,* is a theological term which has been used to express a custom which existed in the early Christian community. Knowledge of the deeper mysteries of Christianity were not only kept from the heathens, but also from those who were undergoing instruction in the Christian faith.[2]

Throughout the reign of the Emperor Nero (54–68 AD) and the reigns of subsequent evil emperors, Christians were commonly persecuted, tortured, or put to death. In fact, it is believed that both Peter and Paul were put to death during Nero's reign.

One of the reasons for worshiping in secret in the first place was because there existed the fear of spies which could betray the Christians and bring about rigid persecution or death. But even for those who shared the faith in "confidence," the ministers who were preaching the gospel would not reveal all the secrets at once. The deeper mysteries were kept from initiates as they were undergoing instruction in the faith to bring them along gradually.

The existence of the *Discipline Of The Secret* concerning heathen or spies could have found its basis in the oral tradition which eventually became the gospel words of Jesus, "Give not what is holy to dogs, nor cast your pearls before swine (MT 7:6)."[3]

The existence of the *Discipline* concerning initiates in whom the Christian community had confidence could have found its basis in the oral tradition which became Paul's Letter to the Corinthians where he speaks about feeding "little ones in Christ." He advises that they should initially be fed "milk and not meat (1Cor 3:1–2)."[4]

The *Discipline of the Secret* also involved a cryptic language used by Christians to communicate with one another. Particularly when the early Christian community wrote to one another, they communicated in the symbolic language of the *Discipline of the Secret*. This was done to conceal its Christian character from the uninitiated. The phraseology is metaphorical.

An example of its use can be found in the Museum of the Lateran Basilica, the mother church of Christendom, in Rome. There exists here, two fragments of an epitaph of a second century Christian of Asia Minor by the name of Abercius. Abercius had his epitaph inscribed in stone as he was dying.

Using the cryptic language of the *Discipline of the Secret*, during the persecutions of his day, Abercius had the following words inscribed on his epitaph:

> Abercius by name. I am the disciple of a venerable shepard..He taught me the faithful scriptures. He sent me to Rome to behold the Sovereign City and to see the Queen in golden raimant and golden shoes. There I saw a people who wear a splendid seal. . . . I found brothers and sisters everywhere. Paul was my companion and everywhere faith led me. Everywhere it served me a fish from the spring, mighty and pure, whom a pure Virgin caught. Without ceasing, she gave fish to friends to eat. She has a delicious wine which she gives with bread.[5]

The words of Abercius, truly express the wonder of his reality in the face of a prevailing mystery. The Church is the people of God, having Christ as their shepherd, baptism as their seal, their faith and the Scriptures as their guide, and the Eucharist for their food.

The *Discipline Of The Secret* seems to have diminished by the fifth century and disappeared entirely within the sixth century. Evidence for the existence of the practice has been documented by many of the fathers of the early church. These would include Tertullian, Basil, Gregory of Nazianzen, Cyril of Jerusalem, Ambrose, Augustine, and John Chrysostom. However, the term itself, *Discipline Of The Secret*, used as such to describe the practice, did not appear until the seventeenth century.

THE MYSTERY FISH

In the early Christian community, one of the symbols that united the primitive Christians was the cross of Jesus Christ. Next to that the *ichthus* symbol, or fish symbol, ranked as one of the most important in unlocking the secrets of the mystery that was Christianity.

The use of the fish symbol in pagan art was of ancient origin. Many of the mystery cults, such as the Cult of Isis had previously employed its usage. Clement of Alexandria is the first early church father to have specifically mentioned the fish symbol (*The Pedagogue 3:11*) as pertaining to Christian usage.[6] He did not give an explanation for its use which seems to imply that the Christian community he was writing to understood the meaning of the symbol. This symbol, first brought to mind in the fledgling Christian community how Jesus had shared a meal of fish with the disciples on the shore of the Sea of Tiberius in Galilee after the resurrection (JN 21:11).[7] But, it had a deeper and more secret meaning.

The fish symbol referenced an acrostic consisting of the initial letters of five Greek words which formed the word for "fish" in the Greek; *ICTYS*, pronounced ICHTHYS. It contained the Greek letters Iota, Chi, Theta, Upsilon, and Sigma. To the early Christian community this signified *Iesous Christos, Theou Yios, Soter* or in the English translation, *Jesus Christ, Son of God, Savior*.[8]

Several representations of the fish symbol can be found on the walls of the catacombs. It initially enabled Christians to identify themselves to each other in secret, without the need for verbal communication; then to proclaim their profession of faith in the divinity of Jesus Christ.

When a Christian met a stranger on the road, he/she would draw one-half of the outline of the fish on a rock or in the dirt. If the stranger drew the other half, both Christian believers knew that they could fellowship and freely share their secret belief in Jesus Christ.

The fish symbol was also scratched on walls or rocks to point the way to where Christians were meeting in secret at ever changing locations. A similar symbol had been utilized by non-Christian Greeks at the time to mark the location of funerals, so the Christian usage blended with that one. The church father, Tertullian would later refer to the early Christians who were being baptized as "Little fishes after the image of our Ichthys, born in water *(Baptism, Tert.1)*."[9]

To early Christians, the symbol of the fish became intimately associated with the resurrected Lord. To them, he was more than a philosophical memory, religious doctrine, or a moral ideal. Jesus was and is a living and present reality.

During the reign of the Emperor Constantine (307–337 AD) the persecution of Christians ceased as he declared Christianity to be the official religion of the state. The fish symbol seems to have disappeared after the fourth century as Christianity spread and the "mysterious secret" of the fish became more widely known to the world. The symbol has been resurrected in more modern times and can be seen displayed everywhere on automobile emblems and bumper stickers.

NOTES

1. Jerome Biblical Commentary, Raymond E. Brown, S.S., Joseph Fitzmeyer, S.J., Roland Murphy, O. Carm., ed., (Englewood Cliffs, NJ: Prentice Hall Publishing, 1968) Sec 41:40–41; 45:31–33; 53:9, 140; 57:21–22; 56:6, 14–15, 19, 38.

2. The New International Encyclopedia, Vol. VI, Daniel C. Gilman, Harry T. Peck, Frank M. Colby, ed., (New York, NY: Dodd Mead & Co., 1906) p. 282. Found online at Googlebooks.com see http://books.google.com/books?id=bjwrAAAAMAAJ&pg=PA282&dq=early+christian+discipline+of+the+secret&hl=en&ei=AMwATdz6MoW_nAe-IdDlDQ&sa=X&oi=book_result&ct =result&resnum=4&ved=0CDwQ6AEwAw#v=onepage&q=early%20christian%20discipline%20of%20the%20secret&f=false.

3. MT 7:6, New American Bible, St. Joseph Edition, Confraternity of Christian Doctrine, Board of Trustees/ National Conference of Catholic Bishops/United States Catholic Conference, Administrative and Editorial Committee/Board (New York, NY: Catholic Book Publishing Co., 1970).

4. 1 Cor 3:1–2, New American Bible, St. Joseph Edition, Confraternity of Christian Doctrine, Board of Trustees/ National Conference of Catholic Bishops/United States Catholic Conference, Administrative and Editorial Committee/Board (New York, NY: Catholic Book Publishing Co., 1970).

5. Abercius/ Discipline of the Secret, The Catholic Encyclopedia, From the New Advent Encyclopedia, found on the New Advent CD-ROM by Kevin Knight (Denver, CO: Advent Internatl, 2009). See also the New Advent website at http://www.newadvent.org/cathen/05032a.htm.

6. Clement of Alexandria, The Pedagogue, Vol. III, ch. 10–11, The Cath. Encyc, From the New Advent Encyclopedia, found on the New Advent CD-ROM by Kevin Knight (Denver, CO: Advent Internatl, 2009). See also the New Advent website at www.NewAdvent.orgfathers/02093.htm.

7. JN 21:11, New American Bible, St. Joseph Edition, Confraternity of Christian Doctrine, Board of Trustees/ National Conference of Catholic Bishops/United States Catholic Conference, Administrative and Editorial Committee/Board (New York, NY: Catholic Book Publishing Co., 1970).

8. Icthys, The Catholic Encyclopedia, From the New Advent Encyclopedia, found on the New Advent CD-ROM by Kevin Knight (Denver, CO: Advent Internatl, 2009). See also the New Advent website at http://www.newadvent.org/cathen/06083a.htm.

9. Tertullian, Baptism, ch. 1, The Catholic Encyclopedia, From the New Advent Encyclopedia, found on the New Advent CD-ROM by Kevin Knight (Denver, CO: Advent Internatl, 2009). See also the New Advent website at http://www.newadvent.org/fathers/0321.htm.

Chapter Eleven

Sacramentality

ALL REALITY IS SYMBOLIC

The Latin word *sacramentum* is a translation of the Greek word *mysterion*. Both can be translated simply as "mystery." When the language of the early Christian Church changed from Greek to Latin, the Greek word *mysterion* was sometimes translated by the Latin word *sacramentum*; it is in this word that we find the biblical roots of the word, "sacrament."[1]

For the first eleven centuries of Christian history the word sacrament was frequently used in this more general sense, referring to the mysterious plan of God. Gradually, specific aspects of this mysterious plan—for example, Baptism, Eucharist, Matrimony, etc.—began to be singled out as rites and called "Sacraments." However, this was not the early usage of the term.

Taking the word "sacrament" in its broadest sense, as the sign of something sacred and hidden, we could say that the whole world is a vast sacramental system, in that material things are unto men the signs of things spiritual and sacred. As Thomas Aquinas has said, "Grace presupposes nature" or "Grace follows nature." Grace is not an add-on. Therefore, a sacrament can be defined simply as "a visible sign of an invisible reality."[2]

This would make the principle of sacramentality to have its rooting in mystery as well as reality. Both reality and mystery are in the first place merely words. But even then, the words themselves become sacramental because they are signifying meaning to us and are more than a group of alphabetized letters.

God is often revealed in images and words, as well as other visible realities, but will always remain more than that. If not, it is not God, but merely an idol. All reality is imbued with the hidden presence of God. Therefore all reality itself is mystery. All reality is a visible sign of an invisible reality, an external sign of something sacred, an outward sign of inward grace, or a natural signal of transcendence.

For example, one might not be able to see the invisible in the visible per se, but we can have an experience of the divine in the human, the Creator in creation, grace in nature, the spiritual in the material, eternity in history, or the sacred in the ordinary.

If all reality is being imbued with the mysterious and hidden presence of God, this would necessarily imply that God can choose to become present to us and reveal Godself to us through other people, events, objects, the world and universe around us, or for that matter anything tangible, visible, or happening in history.

Therefore, because of sacramentality, all reality is ultimately symbolic of mystery and has a hidden character. The mystery that is God, can be seen in virtually everyone and everything around us. Francis of Assisi is a good example of someone who experienced this. Francis saw God mysteriously reflected in the sun, moon, and stars. He saw God in animals, as well as everyone and everything around him.[3]

The greatest Sacrament in both a real and mysterious sense is Jesus Christ. Jesus is the ultimate sign and primal Sacrament of God's presence to us, in us, and through us. That presence will always be veiled and unveiled. It is our response to that presence throughout the course of our lives that concerns our ultimate destiny.

To carry this a step further: If we believe that Jesus is the great Sacrament of God, then that will carry forth into our believing that we, as Christians, here on earth, are the sacrament of Jesus Christ. And this would not be seen only in a narrow ritualistic sense, where the institutional church performs certain public and sacramental acts of the church such as Baptism, Matrimony, etc. These are important for the world to see, but I am speaking about a broader, more personal, more communal experience of the principle of sacramentality. I am speaking of a "sacramental encounter."

What was visible in Jesus public life and ministry has passed over in an invisible way through the Holy Spirit to the life and ministry of Christians on earth. If this becomes real for us, it will become an "actualized mystery" through which Jesus Christ can manifest and reveal His reality.

What this will imply is that others will have a real experience of the mysterious presence of Jesus Christ in us and through us sacramentally. Only God can give the grace for this sacramental encounter with Jesus. If all that is visible and material around us (nature) can convey the mystery of a hidden God, then that should say to us that all reality can be potentially good as it has a sacramental, mysterious character and is essentially "graced nature."

Our God as a God of mystery and majesty is anywhere and everywhere. That should imply that all visible reality can be mediated to us by the unveiling of its meaning to us. But, only God can lift the veil.

NOTES

1. "Sacrament." Douglas Harper, ed., Online Etymology Dictionary. Found online at http://www.etymonline.com/index.php?search=sacrament&searchmode=none (Accessed 12/9/10).
2. Thomas Aquinas, Summa Theologica, Question 2, Article 2, Reply to Obj. 1, From the New Advent Encyclopedia, found on the New Advent CD-ROM by Kevin Knight (Denver, CO: Advent Internatl, 2009). See also the New Advent website at http://www.newadvent.org/summa/1002.htm.
3. Universal History, Eugene Roessenstock-Huessy, ed. (Hanover, NH: Dartmouth College Library, 1997) p. 6. Found online at googlebooks.com. See Googlebooks website at http://books.google.com/books?id=i-hqgce1WX4C&pg=RA8–PA6&dq=Francis+of+assisi+sun+moon+stars+animals&hl=en&ei=0T0BTcq2CaSKnAfmy9TlDQ&sa=X&oi=book_result&ct=result&resnum=7&ved=0CFAQ6AEwBg#v=onepage&q=Francis%20of%20assisi%20sun%20moon%20stars%20animals&f=false.

Chapter Twelve

Revelation: The Unveiling of God

VEILS

In the Old Testament, Exodus 26: 31–37, Moses is told by God how to hang the inner and outer veils which separate the Holy Place and then divide it from the Holy of Holies in the tabernacle. He is told what goes behind the veils and what goes outside them. In the Holy of Holies will rest the Ark of the Covenant and the Ten Commandments with the "Mercy Seat" to be placed on top of the Ark. Then, in Exodus 34: 30–34, we find that Moses had to veil his face because the Israelites were afraid to see it. They could see the brightness of his countenance as his skin had become radiant from conversing with the Lord on Mt. Sinai.

The Temple in Jerusalem was modeled on the dwelling that Moses constructed, as mentioned previously. The veils separated the Holy Place and the Holy of Holies where the High Priest could pass, and then only on the Hebrew celebration of The Day of Atonement (LV 16:1–18).

All three of the Synoptic gospel writers confirm that the veil separating the nave of the Temple from the sanctuary was mysteriously rent in two from top to bottom at the death of Jesus (MT 27:51–53; MK 15: 38; LK 23:45).

The torn veil of the Synoptic gospels is seen to be the inner veil separating the Holy of Holies. The writers see the meaning of this scene to imply that with Jesus' death, all people now have access to the presence of the mystery that is God. And with the Holy of Holies in the Hebrew Temple now being exposed, where it was previously veiled, the Hebrew Temple was now profaned and would soon be destroyed. The writer of Hebrews makes this point as well (HB 9:6–10; 10:19–20).

The Apostle Paul saw all of this in light of the fact that what was "veiled" under the Old Covenant was now giving way to the greater glory of the Gospel of Jesus Christ. This would be the splendor of a New Covenant. He will say that,

> Whenever one turns to the Lord, the veil is removed . . . all of us gazing with unveiled face on the the glory of the Lord are being transformed into the same image from glory to glory, as from the Lord who is the Spirit (2 COR 3:7–18).

Later, Paul would say, "Even though our gospel is veiled, it is veiled for those who are perishing. (2 COR 4:3)."

Finally, it had been prophesied long before all of this by Isaiah (C. 735 BC) that the last veil that would be destroyed by God is the "veil that veils all people . . . "the Lord will destroy death forever" (IS 25:7–8).[1]

Death remains for us, the final earthly reality and the most veiled divine mystery.

REVELATION

God is both veiled and unveiled. In an oxymoronic sense, God can be called both "clearly ambiguous" and "ambiguously clear."

"Revelation," in its literal sense can be defined simply as "the unveiling of God" or "lifting the veil." It is God's self-communication, as mystery, in history. God initiates revelation and those who are open to the mystery of the presence of God, through grace, both recognize and accept that presence in reality.[2]

Faith is not opposed to reason. Faith enfolds and then reason beholds. Through natural reason alone, God can give the grace and man can come to recognize and have faith in the power of God. There does exist, however, a higher knowledge and reality which is hidden in mystery. Man cannot arrive at this mystery through the power of reason alone; this is Divine Revelation. Divine Revelation can only be revealed at God's initiative. Man cannot initiate revelation, man can only, through grace, be receptive to it.

Nothing that is totally inscrutable to reason can be made known to faith. The intellect can only accept those revealed truths whose reasonableness it recognizes. This does not imply that all facets of faith can be readily understood and proven by reason, for there remains the mystery which is contained within Divine revelation. Our human condition contains a finite mind which cannot fully comprehend an infinite God. It is thus through grace and our reasoning powers that we can realize that our reason has limits. To quote Blaise Pascal, "Reason's last step is the recognition that there are an infinite number of things which are beyond it."[3]

The hand of God guides the genius of humankind in searching out the mysteries of the human condition. The guidance God gives is the "inspiration" of

The Holy Spirit. It is a search for unconditional love and truth whose meaning is then unveiled by God and culminates in the unfolding of one of God's mysteries. God reveals some aspect of Godself or the human condition in and through man's search to find the meaning behind the mystery. In man's historical search for God, many people have been inspired, but not everything has been revealed, even many things previously recorded in sacred scripture.

Although God dwells in unapproachable light, God speaks to man by means of the whole universe. Because God is eternal and transcendent (beyond history), and we are located in time and space (in history), revelation is always mediated. We cannot experience God immediately, individually, or directly, even as a mystical experience. Our limited humanity would not allow for this. God's revelation is therefore mediated and can only be experienced sacramentally.

What that implies is that this sacramental encounter can be mediated through another person(s) as symbol, or a thing which is a symbol such as the natural world around us or the Bible as the Word of God. Either way, the God who is shrouded in mystery can lift the veil and "reveal" Godself to us in history. God can give us a "signal of transcendence."[4]

Revelation is, of course, not limited to us at our moment in history, but is occurring within the whole process of history itself. History includes the past, is ongoing, but is thus far incomplete. The deeds wrought by God in the history of the world confirm the reality signified by the words God has revealed in sacred scripture. The words then proclaim the deeds while they reveal the mystery contained in the words. Most particularly, the words reveal the Mystery who is Jesus Christ, the fullness of all revelation. The grace of God can lift the veil, so that through our faith in Jesus Christ we can reach some mediated understanding of this infinite God.

Because God is hidden in mystery, all revelation is sacramental, and mediated by symbols. Jesus Christ, as the Supreme Sacrament of God, mediated and illuminated reality for us in a new way. He essentially gave reality a new meaning in revealing the mystery of who God is. In Jesus, God reveals Godself in history. The resurrection of Jesus is the self-revelation of the living God. Jesus became for us God revealing and God revealed. Jesus Christ was and is the reality of God.

The Divinely revealed reality which is contained in sacred scripture has been committed to writing under the inspiration of the Holy Spirit. It has the God of Mystery as its author, using the real lives and abilities of human beings. And because revelation occurs when the God of Mystery speaks out of silence, it is best perceived and appreciated when the potential hearer of the Word of God is silent for a time before the presence of the mystery.

APOCALYPTICISM

The word, *revelation* is a Latinized word which is translated from the Greek word, *apokalypsis*. They both mean "unveiling" or "lifting the veil." Apocalyptic literature, however, emphasizes more, the hidden plan of a mysterious God. It is a revealed disclosure to privileged persons of something which is hidden from most of humanity.[5] In the Old Testament, the books of Daniel and Ezekiel provided the original pattern for this literature. In the New Testament, we find this type of writing in parts of the Gospels (particularly MK 13), some of Paul's letters (1 THES 4 & 5), and it is most evident in the New Testament Book of Revelation, a.k.a., The Apocalypse of John.[6]

Apocalypticism is a comprehensive name for a style of thought and writing which has an entirely mystical character. It began about 500 BC during Post Exile Judaism and was prevalent from about 200 BC to 100 AD when the Book of Revelation was committed to writing. The style of writing followed the demise of the Old Testament prophets. One can see its beginnings in parts of the book of the prophet Isaiah.

In apocalyptic writing, the imagery breaks the bonds of earthly reality and depicts heaven's secrets. It is rich with mysterious symbolism, fantastic visions, hidden signs, rich allegorical language, as well as predictions of future events and mysterious realities beyond history. All of which would be brought about through the exercise of Divine power as God's sovereign action and intervention.

There are often battles between angelic powers who have cosmic missions. Supernatural forces of good and evil are locked in classic confrontation. An end times (eschatological) victory of good over evil is revealed in symbolic form. There is, in this form of literature, first the unveiling of the mystery of history, then the end of the present era, resurrection of the dead, final judgement, and then the inauguration and emergence of a mysterious Divine Kingdom.

Because apocalyptic literature is said to contain hidden knowledge which is concealed from the average person, it has usually been written during times of crisis and in the face of immense evil. It is persecution as well as underground literature. In our own day, the closest we could come to a modern experience of this type of writing is the many black spirituals which have arisen out of the conditions of slavery in the United States. These would include, *Let My People Go, There Is A Balm In Gilead, Swing Low Sweet Chariot, Marching Around Selma Like Jericho*, and others.

Apocalyptic literature is not meant to be read literally. Because it is timeless, it contains symbolism which can be applied first to the realities which were taking place during the time the writer(s) lived. Only historical criticism can decipher that. But it can also have meaning and import for other times, such as the times we live in today. We should, in fact, be reading the "signs of the times."

In that regard, this literature is very much our reality shrouded in mystery. Its modern meaning and application to our reality cannot be revealed except by the Holy Spirit of God, who remains as not only the God of mystery, but also of history.[7]

NOTES

1. EX 26:31–37; LV 16:1–18; MT 27:51–53; MK 15: 38; LK 23:45; HB 9:6–10; 10:19–20; 2 COR 3:7–18; 2 COR 4:3; IS 25:7–8, New American Bible, St. Joseph Edition, Confraternity of Christian Doctrine, Board of Trustees/ National Conference of Catholic Bishops/United States Catholic Conference, Administrative and Editorial Committee/Board (New York, NY: Catholic Book Publishing Co., 1970).

2. "Reveal." Douglas Harper, ed., Online Etymology Dictionary. Found online at http://www.etymonline.com/index.php?search=reveal&searchmode=none.

3. Peter Kreeft, Christianity for Modern Pagans, (San Fransisco, CA: Ignatius Press, 1993) p. 238.

4. Richard McBrien, Catholicism, (New York, NY: HarperCollins Publishing, 1994) pp. 218–220; 495–499; 522, see also Peter Berger, Rumor of Angels, (Garden City, NY: Doubleday/Anchor Publishing, 1970).

5. "Apocalypse" Douglas Harper, ed., Online Etymology Dictionary. Found online at http://www.etymonline.com/index.php?search=apocalypse&searchmode=none (Accessed12/9/10.

6. 1 THES 4 & 5; Apocalypse of John, New American Bible, St. Joseph Edition, Confraternity of Christian Doctrine, Board of Trustees/ National Conference of Catholic Bishops/United States Catholic Conference, Administrative and Editorial Committee/Board (New York, NY: Catholic Book Publishing Co., 1970).

7. "Apocalyptic." Encyclopedia of Theology, The Concise Sacramentum Mundi, Karl Rahner ed., (New York, NY: Seabury/Crossroads Press, 1975) pp. 16–20 see also Richard McBrien, Catholicism, (New York, NY: HarperCollins Publishing, 1994) pp. 232; 1127–1128; 1135.

Chapter Thirteen
Myth

THE MYSTICAL FUNCTION OF MYTH

When the word, "myth" is used in the New Testament, it is most often used in Paul's letters to refer to false and misleading stories that are dangerous and should be rejected (1TIM 1:4;4:7; 2TIM 4:4; 2PET 1:16).[1] Theologians and scholars use the word in a much more general sense today to refer to the mysteries of the supernatural.

Myth, first of all, has a mystical function where one initially experiences the wonder of the mystery of the universe around us. Myth can then open up the world to the awe that is part of all mysteries where we can visualize how there might be mystery beyond the visible reality. This allows for the transcendent to be experienced both in and beyond the natural world.

The word, "myth" comes from the Greek, *mythos* which is translated as "story."[2] Myth is mystery in the form of a long poem or poetic story. The creation and deluge myths in the book of Genesis are wonderful examples. Just because the book of Genesis contains several myths, that should not imply that the stories it contains are not true in reality. From the beginning of time human beings have created mystical stories to enable them to place their lives in a larger context or setting. These poetic stories suggested that the experience of human life had meaning, purpose, and value. A myth then, could be considered as a poetic story unfolding a world view and describing the mystery of life. It is a poet's view of reality.

A poetic story told in the form of myth makes an attempt to explain a reality that is steeped in mystery. So, when something is said to be a myth it doesn't mean that it is unreal, irrational, or untrue. Myths describe important mysteries that must be written in poetic language because ordinary language can't describe these realities nearly as well. This would include, for example, giving answers to questions which would describe mysterious realities, such as the relationship between the divine and humans, creation, afterlife, the first humans, end times etc. Mythology through its poetry usually speaks of another mysterious world alongside this world.

Myth gives shape and form to another world of reality that is sensed intuitively and expressed poetically through the human spirit. As poetry, the words of myth are preferential in explaining and discussing these mysterious realities because the words of prose would not render the understanding as adequately. The subject matter is beyond reason and logic alone.

If a "dream" can be defined as "an unconscious expression of an individual reality," myth could be called "collective dreaming" as it embodies society's dream or a collective consciousness of reality. The human mind by its very nature is imaginative. We as humans have ideas that cannot be expressed logically or rationally. Our mind enables us to think of ideas or concepts which are not immediately present or real to us. It is imagination through inspiration which produces the mysterious poetry that is mythology.

Myth uses much symbolism and imagery as well as figurative and allusive language to tell its story. Like most poetry, its language is subtle, vague, and mysterious. Symbols are emblems of reality and truth; they have significance and meaning. The function of a symbol in myth is to be the vehicle for communicating reality. The symbol often embodies an idea and should not be mistaken for the reality itself or for what or to whom the symbol is making reference. The reality is always beyond that stated literally in the words and remains shrouded in mystery.

The symbols of myth are always transparent or translucent and should never block the light they are trying to reflect. A symbol often suggests someone or something by reason of the relationship. Words that depict certain people, communities, movements, events, places, objects, or parts of the world or cosmos, as used in myth, can often be symbolic of something or someone else in their usage.

A wedding ring, for example, is only a round piece of gold, but it is first and foremost a symbol of marriage. Then it has a deeper significance in that it is a symbol of lifelong commitment and everlasting love. It may even be symbolic of deeper sacramental realities which are not now immediately present to our consciousness and wrapped in a mystery that transcends this earthly life.

Myth seeks to impose intelligible form upon the reality that transcends human experience. This reality is expressed by symbolic representation which is drawn from the existing realm of human experience. Myth gives us insight into the reality which is beyond our immediate understanding or which cannot be grasped by strictly logical explanations. The stories of myth harmonize our lives with reality. To experience the symbols of myth is to experience the sensual, aesthetic, spiritual, intellectual, emotional, and evocative dimensions of poetry. The symbols utilized never become the reality, but they do give insight into both the reality and the mystery to which they point.

One of the greatest mythologists of our generation was Joseph Campbell, now deceased. My favorite of all his quotes is "Follow your bliss!"[3]

In his ground-breaking book, *The Power Of Myth,* Joseph Campbell states,

> Poetry is a language that has to be penetrated. Poetry involves a precise choice of words that will have implications and suggestions that go past the words themselves. Then you experience the radiance, the epiphany; the epiphany is the showing through the essence.[4]

Whenever the mystery of God is totally demythologized through philosophical thought and the exercise of pure reason, then we lose insight into the reality of God as well. Therefore, myth is the best expression of that reality we call "transcendent" or the "mystery of God." This being a reality which is outside the scope of our limited human intelligence, logic, and reason.[5]

Finally, the meaning of a symbol in myth is never absolute and is often dictated by the culture surrounding the writer. Therefore, myth, as a poetic story, must be looked at through the eyes of historical criticism and in the context and setting in which it was written. This would apply no matter whether we were reading the biblical books of *Genesis* and *Revelation*,[6] Homer's *Odyssey*,[7] Milton's *Paradise Lost*,[8] or any mythology for that matter. For example, I might write a story today which has a line that reads, "It was raining cats and dogs." One should not imagine reading the story years from now that cats and dogs were literally falling from the sky today.

NOTES

1. 1TIM 1:4;4:7; 2TIM 4:4; 2PET 1:16, New American Bible, St. Joseph Edition, Confraternity of Christian Doctrine, Board of Trustees/ National Conference of Catholic Bishops/United States Catholic Conference, Administrative and Editorial Committee/Board (New York, NY: Catholic Book Publishing Co., 1970).

2. "Myth." Douglas Harper, ed., Online Etymology Dictionary. Found online at http://www.etymonline.com/index.php?search=myth&searchmode=none (Accessed 12/10/10).

3. Joseph Campbell, The Hero's Journey, Stuart Brown, ed. (Novato CA: New World Library Publications, 1990) p. 217.

4. Joseph Campbell, The Power of Myth, Betty Flowers, ed., (New York, NY: Anchor Books/Doubleday, 1991).

5. Richard McBrien, Catholicism, (New York, NY: HarperCollins Publishing, 1994) pp. 218–220; 495–499; 522.

6. New American Bible, St. Joseph Edition, Confraternity of Christian Doctrine, Board of Trustees/ National Conference of Catholic Bishops/United States Catholic Conference, Administrative and Editorial Committee/Board (New York, NY: Catholic Book Publishing Co., 1970).

7. Homer, The Odyssey, Elliot Sokolov, Amie Brockway-Henson, ed., (Woodstock, IL: Dramatic Publishing, 1998).

8. John Milton, Paradise Lost, Elijah Fenton, Samuel Johnson, ed., (London, Eng.: John Bumpus Co., Cambridge, MA: Harvard College Library, 1821).

Chapter Fourteen
Old Testament Mystery

THE DREAMERS

In the scriptures, the Old-Testament uses the Greek word, *mysterion,* as an equivalent translation for the Hebrew "sôd," "secret." The word was also translated from the Aramaic "raza" which evolved from the Persian word "raz" which meant "secret." Raza was used most often to designate an end-time or eschatological secret yet to be revealed by God. The term is used frequently in the Old Testament apocalyptic Book of Daniel.[1]

In the Pentateuch, God first reveals Godself in creation.[2] Man, contemplating the mystery of the created world and reflecting upon it, can potentially perceive through its veil, the great unseen reality behind it. One can sense the mystery of the divine character and loving personhood of its Creator. Though mysteriously invisible, the Maker is mirrored in the works of his hand.

The revelation of His mysterious reality occurs in history as a developing process and insight into His character grows through the successive periods of Israel's history. Yahweh is then recognized as a God of mystery who cannot be known further except through the revelation of words and deeds. The words and deeds of Yahweh communicate a knowledge of the kind of God He is which is personally and communally experienced by the Israelites. This knowledge is not like having the personal experience of any other person. In many instances, when the Israelite had a knowledge of Yahweh, this implied that they would carry out the revealed will of Yahweh. The response to the mystery was to submit obediently.[3]

Chapter Fourteen

There are several occasions throughout the Old Testament where God continues to reveal the mystery of His divine reality. Some of these are as follows:

- God appears to Abraham (GEN 17:1–27) and God reveals Himself to Jacob at Bethel (Gen 35:7).
- He appears to Moses in the burning bush and reveals his name as "I Am Who I Am/Yahweh." God gives Moses his calling, mission and the promise to lead the Israelites out of Egypt (EX: ch 1–18); then reveals the covenant at Mount Sinai and the Ten Commandments to Moses (EX: ch 19–24).
- God reveals Himself to Moses (LV 9:4–23; 10:3; 16:2); Aaron and Miriam (NM 12:6; SIR 45:3); and then later to Samuel (1 SAM 3:1–10).
- Later in Israel's history, He reveals Himself and the mystery of His reality through the prophets (IS: 40:5; 53:1; 56:1). The prophets will also tell us that He has hidden knowledge to reveal when He chooses and to whom He chooses (IS 48:3; Amos 3:7). God sometime delivered this hidden knowledge in person (GEN 17; EX 3) and sometimes through an angel or messenger (GEN 22).
- God does reveal Himself through many miracles in the Old Testament. These will be discussed in a separate section of the book under the heading, "The Miracles Mystery."

But, perhaps one of the more mysterious ways God reveals Himself in the Old Testament is through individuals he appoints as key interpreters of dreams. The two major figures he chooses to reveal Himself through dreams are the patriarch Joseph and the young man Daniel.

In Genesis, chapters 40 and 41, Joseph, by the grace of God, is given the power first, to correctly interpret the dreams of Pharaoh's royal cup bearer and his baker. Then, while wrongfully in prison, he is called by Pharaoh, whose magicians cannot interpret Pharaoh's own two dreams of seven fat and seven skinny cows. When brought into Pharaoh's presence and asked to interpret his dreams, Joseph responds, "It is not I, but God, who will give Pharaoh the right answer (Gen. 41:16)."

Joseph proceeds to interpret Pharaoh's dreams of the fat and skinny cows to mean that there will be seven years of plenty and seven years of famine throughout the land of Egypt. Ultimately, Pharaoh responds to Joseph, "Since God has made all this known to you, no one can be as wise and discerning as you are. You will be in charge of my palace . . . (Gen 41:39–40)." In the end, Pharaoh comes to recognize the divine origin of the revelation of the mystery.

The second instance where this can be seen most vividly is in the Old Testament Book of Daniel, as King Nebuchadnezzar asks Daniel the meaning of his dream, to which the king's wise men, enchanters, magicians, and astrologers could not provide an answer. God reveals these mysteries to Daniel which allow him to answer the king and proceed to explain the mysteries. Daniel says, "There is a God in heaven who reveals mysteries and He has shown King Nebuchadnezzar what is to happen in days to come . . . To me also, this mystery has been revealed."

Daniel proceeds to describe the meaning of the multi-metal statue and unhewn stone which shatters it in the king's dream as representing certain future kingdoms. Ultimately, the king responds to Daniel by saying, "Truly, your God is the God of gods and Lord of kings and a revealer of mysteries; that is why you were able to reveal this mystery (Dan 2: 28–47)."

There is no greater human mystery than death. The Old Testament prophet, Isaiah, foresees an end someday and a revelation to even this great mystery when he says, "On this mountain, the Lord of Hosts will destroy the veil that veils all peoples, the web that is woven over all nations; He will destroy death forever (IS 25:7)."[4] The mountain is, of course, Zion, the symbol of the heavenly Jerusalem.

VEILED VOICES: THE PROPHETS

To human persons, the future is shrouded in mystery. A prophet is one who utters divinely inspired revelations and in doing so, often not only preaches, but also mysteriously foretells the future. Prophets are inspired poets and spiritual seers who posses mystical knowledge of future events as they serve as intermediaries between God and the people of God. Every prophet is like unto Moses: "Then the Lord put forth his hand and touched my mouth; and the Lord said to me "Behold I have put my words in your mouth (Jer 1:9)."[5]

The Hebrew word, *nabi*, is loosely translated as "prophet" and it means literally "one who announces." Prophets were the conscience of Israel, unveiling the mind and will of God. In the Old Testament body of literature, *The Writings of the Prophets*, are considered to be the second part of the Hebrew Scriptures. The Prophets account for ½ of the Old Testament books.

There arose, in Israel, Major Prophets, such as Isaiah, Jerimiah, and Ezekial and those called Minor Prophets, such as Hosea, Joel, Amos, Obadiah, Jonah, Micah, Nahum, Habakkuk, Zephaniah, Haggai, Zecariah, and Malachi. The prophets of Israel are not confined to the second part of the Hebrew Scriptures as many so-called Former Prophets, had paved the way for them. These would include Abraham, Moses, Samuel, Elijah, and David. There were also several women who were considered prophetesses such as Sarah, Miriam, Deborah, Esther, and Huldah.

As messengers, they were all veiled voices of God who spoke in season and out of season. In addition to preaching God's word, they also proclaimed oracles and visions of the future within the context of revelation, never bullying or threatening, but often only warning. They stood over against their own society as both critics and judges for the good of their community.

The prophets were accredited by signs (Is 7: 11,14) and by the ensuing fulfillment of what had been their predictions, as the future was made the present (Dt 18: 21–22). Essentially there came the realization in time of what had originally been their foretold mysteries. A prime Old Testament example of this was many of the prophets' foretelling of the coming Exile of the people of Israel and their eventual rescue and restoration (Is 5:11–13, 38:5–6, 39:6–7; Jer 20:6, 25:11; Amos 1:5, 7:9–17; Mic 4:10).

Christians also believe that several Old Testament prophecies were fulfilled in the coming of Jesus Christ. A prime example of this would be the "suffering servant" passages of Isaiah being fulfilled first by the people of Israel, then in the coming of Jesus Christ 700 years after these passages were written (Is 52:13–53:12).

Revelation (lifting the veil), cannot be confined to a particular time in history. It occurs within the entire historical process itself. Therefore, the mystery that surrounds all prophecy cannot be treated as if it were entirely complete. There are always deeper prophetic mysteries than the mystery seen to be already revealed by the Old Testament prophets which can be found in our reading the "signs of the times."

Finally, we are told in the Old Testament Book of Sirach, one of the Wisdom Books of the Bible, that wisdom is necessary to understand any mystery (Sir 1:5; 20:29–30).[6] We can never have enough wisdom to understand and fully grasp the mysteries of God. So, the God in heaven who reveals mysteries must see to it that Lady Wisdom really has HER hold on us.

THE MYSTIQUE OF LADY WISDOM

Throughout the Old Testament of the Bible, we see a mysterious character emerge who we can simply call "Lady Wisdom"/ *Hokmah* in the Hebrew. Although God is mostly described and depicted in very Patriarchal terms in the Old Testament, wisdom, on the other hand, is personified as a "She." This whole idea was illustrated extensively in Chapter Two (*Wisdom In Person*, pp. 20–32) of my first book, *GET WISDOM*.[7]

In the earliest books of the Old Testament, wisdom in the broadest sense implied skill or expertise. It was seen as something utilitarian which was used to teach people how to lead happy lives. In the earlier books, wisdom was seen to belong on the human level and not revealed as an attribute of God. The ancients who were seen to cultivate wisdom were called "sages."

At the time of the writing of the Wisdom Literature, beginning with the Book of Job (500 BC), The characteristics of wisdom took on a more divine, religious, and ethical nature. At this time a "theology of wisdom" began to appear as the transcendence of wisdom was revealed (Jb 28). God would be associated with divine wisdom as a characteristic inherent in God's creative ability. At this time, the personification of wisdom began, as outlined in the Old Testament Wisdom Literature *(Job, Proverbs, Ecclesiastes, Sirach, Book of Wisdom)*.

Here wisdom would be portrayed as a pre-existent person; God's mysterious first person with prophetic and divine traits. She would stand apart from God, have an intermediate role in creation, and in the government and ordering of the universe. She was seen to have twenty-one personal attributes that were outlined in the Old Testament Book of Wisdom. They were as follows . . .

1. Intelligence
2. Holiness
3. Uniqueness
4. Manifold
5. Subtleness
6. Agility
7. Clarity
8. Without blemish
9. Certainty
10. Not Baneful
11. Loving the good (Wis 7:22–23)
12. Keenness
13. Unhampered
14. Beneficence
15. Kindness
16. Firmness
17. Security
18. Tranquility
19. Omnipotence
20. All-seeing
21. Pervading all spirits

Although the above Biblical reference best describes the "personality" of wisdom, the following scripture references describe her nature as this mysteriously hidden "she" begins to emerge from within a very patriarchal culture.

1. Wisdom is personified as "She" (Prov 1–9; Sir 4:11–19, 6:18–31, 14:20–15:8; Bar 3:9–4:4; Wis 6:12–11:1).
2. Her origins are divine (Prov 8:22; Sir 24:3, 9; Wis 7:25–26).
3. She was pre-existent and had a role in creation (Prov 8:22–29; Sir 1:4,9–10; Wis 7:22, 8:4–6, 9:9).
4. She is identified with the divine spirit/imminent in the world (Wis 1:7, 7:28, 8:1, 9:17, 12:1).
5. She promises life (Prov 3:2, 16–18, 9:11).[8]

The fact that Lady Wisdom is described in the feminine should not be construed to diminish one of the coming earthly roles of Jesus Christ as "the Wisdom of God (1Cor 1:24)." It should be viewed as further adding to the mystery of the human person. Jesus was divine.

Being divine implies then, that Jesus was also a perfect human being. As a perfect human being, Jesus would have been a fully sexually integrated human being as well.

Lady Wisdom should be seen as a divine communication; God's mysterious self-communication. Jesus can and should be seen as HumanDivine; at once both male and wisdom incarnate.

Later, the New Testament Gospel writer, John, will show us this when he does not refer to Jesus as *Sophia/Wisdom* in the Greek, but as *Logos/Word* in the Greek. "In the beginning (JN 1:1)" is language that harkens back to the Old Testament book of Genesis. In using the term, *Logos*, John is telling us that Jesus is not only the embodiment of the wisdom described in female terms in both the Hebrew and Greek religious traditions (*Hokmah and Sophia*). He is also the instrument of God's dynamic, creative word and activity and the personified, pre-existent wisdom as the instrument of God's creative activity (Old Testament Book of Proverbs). And finally, using the term *Logos* is also saying to all of the followers of Hellenistic philosophy, that this same GodMan/ Jesus is furthermore, the ultimate revelation of all intelligible reality. Essentially and existentially, Jesus reveals the mystery of God's reality; for he is God revealing, God revealed, God realizing, God realized.[9]

SECRET OF THE DIVINE NAME

In the Near East, great significance was attached to personal names. Names revealed character and identity, indicated who the person was, and how they conducted themselves. The revelation of the secret of the divine name was of great importance to many ancient cultures because it was believed to be the means by which the deity could be known. The aforementioned ancient Cult of Isis is a prime example.

In Hebrew thought, "to know God," was to encounter the personal reality who is God. But, a person cannot be known unless their name is known. In the Hebrew language there is an association between the person and the name which is unlike our language. Where the Hebrew language might use the word "name," we might use "person" or "self." If one had no name, one did not exist. In other words, one had no basis or existence in reality. To "know" the name was to then "know" the reality named.

The name *YAHWEH*, (Hebrew characters יהוה), in the form of the four consonant letters "YHWH," is usually transliterated from the Hebrew as *I Am Who Am*. The name appears to connote divine mystery and signifies God's real presence. The name held the key to the revelation of a secret, i.e. who God is.[10]

The revelation of the divine name to Israel, through Moses, (EX 3:13–15) represented a revelation of the personal reality of *Yahweh*. The name would indicate that He would be a personal God and could be proclaimed as the personal Divine Being who reveals Himself to Israel. The name revealed God as the absolute and necessary being; the source of all created beings. His mysterious essence would not be shared by any other being. To the Israelite, God would be present and active wherever and whenever the name was known and invoked. To know the name was to know *Yahweh* (IS 52:6; 64:1). To call upon the name was to come before the mystery and into the presence of God.

Eventually came the realization in the Jewish community that the personal reality of *Yahweh*, who is, did not lie within the limited comprehension of man, for *Yahweh* is also a God of unfathomable mystery as well. The Israelites had been told, for example, that "My thoughts are not your thoughts" and "My ways are not your ways (IS 55:8–9)."[11]

Although the name was a key to unlocking the mystery, the mystery remained ongoing. *Yahweh* remained transcendent and infinitely above everything we could fully know or say about the meaning of the name. In many ways he is still the hidden God whose name is ineffable. In the presence of the mystery, the only proper attitude is humble submission and recognition of one's own limited human intelligence. In this life we will not know more about the meaning of the secret name than we will know.

From about the time of the destruction of the Jewish temple in 70 AD, there developed great respect for the secretness and sanctity of the name of God amongst the Hebrews. There came a time in their history that they would not pronounce the name and would use in its place *Adonai*, which is translated from the Hebrew as *My Lord*, or *Elohim*, the Hebrew word for *God*. There were also various forms of *El* used, most particularly *El Shaddai*, translated as *Almighty God*.

The modern rendering of the name *Jehovah* as the English translation of the divine name is incorrect. It is a bad translation of the original Hebrew text. It comes from adding vowels to the four consonants YHWH when translating into English.

The name *Jesus* represents a Hellenized form of the Hebrew name, *Yeshua*. Jesus name in the Hebrew also indicates a revelation of His character and identity. The name *Yeshua* is translated *Yahweh Is Salvation*. Similar to the manner in which the sanctity of the personal name of God had developed among the ancient Israelites in referring to *Yahweh* simply as *Adonai/my Lord*, later in the writing of the New Testament, the early Christian community would apply the Greek name and title, *Kyrios*, translated as *my Lord*, to the risen Christ (ACTS 2:36; 7:59).[12]

NOTES

1. Jerome Biblical Commentary, Raymond E. Brown, S.S., Joseph Fitzmeyer, S.J., Roland Murphy, O. Carm., ed., (Englewood Cliffs, NJ: Prentice Hall Publishing, 1968) Sec 26:15.

2. "Pentateuch." Genesis, Exodus, Leviticus, Numbers, Deuteronomy, New American Bible, St. Joseph Edition, Confraternity of Christian Doctrine, Board of Trustees/ National Conference of Catholic Bishops/United States Catholic Conference, Administrative and Editorial Committee/Board (New York, NY: Catholic Book Publishing Co., 1970).

3. Richard McBrien, Catholicism, (New York, NY: HarperCollins Publishing, 1994) pp. 279–280. see also Jerome Biblical Commentary, Raymond E. Brown, S.S., Joseph Fitzmeyer, S.J., Roland Murphy, O. Carm., ed., (Englewood Cliffs, NJ: Prentice Hall Publishing, 1968) Sec 11:12; 14:2; 15:3, 4, 30; 19:19. 84; 20:10; 22:12, 15; 77:96, 106, 117.

4. GEN 17:1–27; Gen 35:7; EX: ch 1–18;EX: ch 19–24; LV 9:4–23;10:3; 16:2; NM 12:6; SIR 45:3; 1 SAM 3:1–10; IS: 40:5; 53:1; 56:1; IS 48:3; Amos 3:7; EN 17; EX 3; GEN 22; GEN ch. 40; 41; Dan 2: 28–47; IS 25:7, New American Bible, St. Joseph Edition, Confraternity of Christian Doctrine, Board of Trustees/National Conference of Catholic Bishops/United States Catholic Conference, Administrative and Editorial Committee/Board (New York, NY: Catholic Book Publishing Co., 1970).

5. Jer 1:9, New American Bible, St. Joseph Edition, Confraternity of Christian Doctrine, Board of Trustees/ National Conference of Catholic Bishops/United States Catholic Conference, Administrative and Editorial Committee/Board (New York, NY: Catholic Book Publishing Co., 1970).

6. Jerome Biblical Commentary, Raymond E. Brown, S.S., Joseph Fitzmeyer, S.J., Roland Murphy, O. Carm., ed., (Englewood Cliffs, NJ: Prentice Hall Publishing, 1968) Sec 12: 1–25; 66:9; 67:20–28; 77:107. See also The Prophetic Books, New American Bible, St. Joseph Edition, Confraternity of Christian Doctrine, Board of Trustees/ National Conference of Catholic Bishops/United States Catholic Conference, Administrative and Editorial Committee/Board (New York, NY: Catholic Book Publishing Co., 1970) pp. 822–823.

7. Michael A. Hickey, Get Wisdom, (Philadelphia, PA: Xlibris Publishing, 2006) pp. 20–32.

8. The Wisdom Books, New American Bible, St. Joseph Edition, Confraternity of Christian Doctrine, Board of Trustees/ National Conference of Catholic Bishops/ United States Catholic Conference, Administrative and Editorial Committee/Board (New York, NY: Catholic Book Publishing Co., 1970) pp. 701–823. See also Roland E. Murphy, The Tree of Life, 2nd edition (Grand Rapids, MI: Eeerdmans Publishing, 1990) pp. 27; 79; 133–149.

9. Jerome Biblical Commentary, Raymond E. Brown, S.S., Joseph Fitzmeyer, S.J., Roland Murphy, O. Carm., ed., (Englewood Cliffs, NJ: Prentice Hall Publishing, 1968) Sec 80:21–24; 63:1–85.

10. Jerome Biblical Commentary, Raymond E. Brown, S.S., Joseph Fitzmeyer, S.J., Roland Murphy, O. Carm., ed., (Englewood Cliffs, NJ: Prentice Hall Publishing, 1968) Sec 3:12; 77:11–14.

11. EX 3:13–15; IS 52:6; 64:1; IS 55:8–9, New American Bible, St. Joseph Edition, Confraternity of Christian Doctrine, Board of Trustees/ National Conference of Catholic Bishops/United States Catholic Conference, Administrative and Editorial Committee/Board (New York, NY: Catholic Book Publishing Co., 1970).

12. Richard McBrien, Catholicism, (New York, NY: HarperCollins Publishing, 1994) pp. 279–280. See also Jerome Biblical Commentary, Raymond E. Brown, S.S., Joseph Fitzmeyer, S.J., Roland Murphy, O. Carm., ed., (Englewood Cliffs, NJ: Prentice Hall Publishing, 1968) Sec 3:12; 77:11–14.

Chapter Fifteen

New Testament Mystery

MYSTERY HAS SEVERAL DIFFERENT NAMES

Until the writing of the New Testament, the last time the word *mysterion* or *mystery* appears anywhere in the scriptures is in the Old Testament book of Daniel. It doesn't appear in any of the writings of either the major or minor prophets. The word *mysterion* or *mystery* then appears 27 times in the New Testament. It denotes not so much the meaning of the modern English term "mystery," but rather something that is mystical. In the biblical Greek, the term refers to "that which, being outside of natural human powers of logic, reason, intelligence, or apprehension, and can be made known only by Divine Revelation."

Mysterion or *mystery* is known by several different names in the New Testament:

The *mystery* of the kingdom (MT 13:11)
The *mystery* of God, Christ (Col 2:2)
The *mystery* of God's will (EPH 1:9)
The *mystery* of Christ (EPH 3:4)
The *mystery* of the gospel (EPH 6:19)
The *mystery* of the faith (1 TIM 3:9)
The *mystery* of devotion (1 TIM 3:16)
The hidden wisdom of God's *mystery* (1COR 2:7)[1]

SYNOPTIC GOSPELS

In the New Testament the word mystery is then often applied to the revealed truths of the sublime revelation of the Gospel. In the Synoptic gospels, for example, when the disciples approach Jesus and ask why he speaks in parables, Jesus says to them in reply, "Because knowledge of the mysteries of the kingdom of heaven has been granted to you, but to them it has not been granted. To anyone who has, more will be given and he will grow rich" (MT 13:11).

Similar statements concerning the mystery of the kingdom appear in Mark and Luke as well (MK 4:11; LK 8:10). In rabbinical literature there were over 2000 parables which were told in answer to the questions of a disciple. Jesus, in the gospels, is depicted as using a similar approach. A parable was typically used as a figure of speech to compare things to illustrate a religious principle. It demands contemplation and reflection for understanding. Only those who are prepared to understand its meaning can come to know it and consequently know the mysteries of the kingdom Jesus is speaking about. Both the disciples' understanding of the mystery and the crowd's inability to grasp it are attributed to God.

"Knowledge of the mysteries of the kingdom," implies a recognition that the Kingdom has become present in one's midst in the life and public ministry of Jesus of Nazareth. It is used to designate God's divine plan for the unfolding of the Kingdom in the course of history that can only be known when revealed. God will grant more understanding to one who acknowledges and accepts the revealed mystery. To the crowd, Jesus presents the Kingdom in parables and the truths of the mystery remain hidden to them.[2]

PAUL'S LETTERS

Collossians 2:2–3

"... they are brought together in love to have all the richness of fully assured understanding, for the knowledge of the mystery of God, Christ, in whom are hidden all the treasures of wisdom and knowledge."

Most scripture scholars agree that Colossians is an authentic Pauline letter and part of the Apostle Paul's original gospel. This was not questioned in the early church at all and the church father Irenaeus accepted it as canonical early on. In the letter to the Colossians as well as well as the letter to the Ephesians (EPH 1:9), Paul will strongly emphasize that the mystery he is proclaiming in his gospel is not a "secret" which is reserved for just a few privileged initiates (as was the case with all the mystery cults discussed earlier). This mystery is rather destined for the entire world.

Some scripture scholars also believe that Paul's usage of the word *mysterion* may have been intentionally aimed at the contemporary mystery cults who would have been familiar with the term. Paul believes that the power and authority of the Gospel of Christ needs to be proclaimed world-wide and is somehow working in him in a mighty way. In Christ are hidden all the treasures of wisdom and knowledge. Paul sees himself as contained within the mystery he is sharing. He sees himself as a guardian or steward who dispenses the wealth of the mystery (1 COR 4: 1).

1 Timothy 3:9

"Deacons must be dignified, not deceitful, not addicted to drink, not greedy for sordid gain, holding fast to the mystery of faith . . ."

In addition to having dignity and practicing the virtue of temperance, deacons must hold fast to the mystery of the revealed truths of the sublime revelation of the gospel. The mystery describes the secret that was hidden in Divine Wisdom in all the earlier centuries and only revealed through Jesus Christ. This "secret" within the mystery is that the redemption of all mankind (not just a privileged few) is accomplished by Christ and can be obtained through a faith-filled union with Christ.

1 Corinthians 15:51

"Behold, I tell you a mystery. We shall not all fall asleep, but we will all be changed, in an instant, in the blink of an eye, at the last trumpet."

This part of the mystery is now disclosed, the very last moment in God's plan is revealed. Paul had begun to discuss other facets of this mystery at the beginning of his letter to the Corinthians. Paul will identify this mystery and equate it with the gospel. He will speak about the mystery as being "Jesus Christ Crucified (1 Cor 2:1–10)." The pattern of God's secret has been hidden from others, but now revealed to the church; God's Divine Wisdom: His plan for our salvation and the manner of the resurrection.

The Divine plan of salvation is mysteriously being realized in Christ Jesus. At the last moment in the history of the world, the trumpet will sound and the dead will be raised. Any who happen to be alive at that moment along with the dead will be transformed. At that time, God will provide glorified man with a body suitable for his glorious state. What kind of a body that will be remains a mystery yet to be revealed.

The Incarnation: The mystery is also applied to the Incarnation and life of Jesus Christ as Saviour and then later to His manifestation by the preaching of the Apostles.

Romans 11:25; 16:25

"I do not want you to be unaware of this mystery . . ."

"Now to Him who can strengthen you according to my gospel and the proclamation of Jesus Christ, according to the revelation of the mystery kept secret for long ages . . ."

In saying, "my gospel," Paul is speaking about the good news he is making known in his preaching of Jesus Christ. Paul's gospel here reveals the mystery which was kept secret for many long ages past: justification and salvation through faith in Jesus Christ. The mystery now revealed begins with the command of the Eternal God, is manifested in the life and incarnation of Jesus Christ, and then ends with ongoing faith in Him.

Ephesians 1:9–10; 3:4–5; 6:19

"He has made known to us the mystery . . ."

"When you read this, you can understand my insight into the mystery of Christ which was not made known to human beings of other generations, as it has now been revealed to His holy apostles and prophets by the Spirit . . ."

"That speech may be given to me to open my mouth to make known with boldness the mystery of the gospel . . ."

Paul is writing from prison. This mystery which is being revealed in Paul's gospel first focuses on God's Divine plan to deliver Gentiles along with Jews through Jesus Christ as co-partners, with one head, to sum up all things in Christ. In Colossians, the mystery Paul will speak about will refer to the hidden presence and working of Jesus Christ. Here, in Ephesians, Paul is using mystery in a different sense to refer to the revelation of the previously hidden plan of God concerning the deliverance of both Jews and Gentiles.

Colossians 1:26; 4:3

"To bring to completion for you the word of God, the mystery hidden from ages and from generations past . . ."

"Pray for us, too, that God may open a door to us for the word, to speak of the mystery of Christ."

The revelation of the mystery Paul speaks about is the preaching of the gospel, so that God's Word will carry out His Divine Plan and make Jesus Christ known to the Gentiles. It essentially teaches the God-given wisdom about Christ: Christ in us, as our hope of future glory. Christ will ultimately reveal the mystery which is Himself; His presence in us. Until then, He remains hidden in mankind.[3]

THE BOOK OF REVELATION

The Book of Revelation, also called, "The Apocalyse of John," is the only complete apocalyptic book of the New Testament. There are certain verses, however, which are considered to be apocalyptic in the gospels and epistles of the New Testament (ex. Mk 13; 1 Thes 4 & 5). This book is an "unveiling."

As was stated previously, the word *apokalupsis*, from the Greek, as well as our own word *revelation*, literally means an, "unveiling."

Apocalypses have to do directly with mysteries and their meaning. In that sense, The Book of Revelation is doubly mysterious. First, because it is apocalyptic and its intended meaning is hidden from most of humanity. Second, because the book is prophetic, and as such, it deals in part with the future, which is unknown and a mystery to human persons. We are told this immediately from the book's opening words: "The revelation of Jesus Christ, which God gave him to show his servants what must soon take place; and he made it known by sending his angel to his servant John, . . ." (Rev 1:1).

The book contains much poetic imagery, rich allegory, and myth, as well as many symbols which are intended to reveal meaning. The language, however, because it is so metaphorical, symbolic, and mysterious is extremely difficult to easily interpret. There are many oblique references. A close reading of the Old Testament books of Daniel and Ezekial does help here, as much of the symbolism in The Book of Revelation was drawn from those books, particularly the Old Testament apocalyptic Book of Daniel.

This book is also filled with considerable numerology. What all the numbers mean exactly is somewhat vague as they also contain layers of hidden meaning. The number 7, in particular, holds special significance and is symbolically considered by many to represent perfection, completeness and totality as opposed to an exact categorical number. The book consists of 7 different visions which are themselves divided into 7 different parts. There are 7 letters to 7 churches, as well as 7 angels (Rev 1–3), 7 torches representing 7 spirits (Rev 4:5), a scroll sealed with 7 seals (Rev 5:1–2), a Lamb of God with 7 horns and 7 eyes (Rev 5:6), 7 trumpted judgements heralded by 7 angels (Rev 8–11), 7 thunders where nothing is said (Rev 10:3), a red dragon with 7 heads having 7 crowns (Rev 12:3), and 7 plagues of God's wrath unleashed by the 7th trumpet and poured out by 7 angels of God (Rev 15:11).

Although there are numerous and varied interpretations of the exact meaning of all of the mysteries contained within this apocalyptic book, there are a few things which are clear and certain. There is no doubt that the victory will be God's. God will be victorious and defeat God's enemies, including Satan. And God's faithful will be rewarded with a new heaven and earth.

As at the beginning of time, the archangel Michael will appear at the end of time to be God's servant in the battle between good and evil and will worship the Lamb of God, Jesus Christ, on his throne. As the writer of the Book of Revelation states:

> Now war arose in heaven, Michael and his angels fighting against the dragon; and the dragon and his angels fought, but they were defeated and there was no longer any place for them in heaven. And the great dragon was thrown down,

that ancient serpent, who is called the Devil and Satan, the deceiver of the whole world-he was thrown down to earth, and his angels were thrown down with him (Rev 12:7–14).

The Book of Revelation is not chronological. It deals with events past, present, and future. As past, it was originally written and focused on events involving the persecution of Christians during the time of the reign of the evil Roman emperors Nero and Domitian (68–95 AD). But, it should also be read with an eye to similar events which might be unfolding today. We should always be attempting to read "the signs of the times." On the other hand, the book was never written and intended to be read as a literal interpretation of any particular or static moment in time, including our current place in the historical process. Mystery is beyond any moment in time and history is unfinished and incomplete for us. But, to God the future is always present.

The book culminates with the tribulation of the last years of mankind, the second coming of Christ, and the establishment of his reign on earth. The book ends with the words of Jesus and the final affirmation of the writer. It is a fitting end, not only to the Book of Revelation, but the entire Bible as well: "Surely I am coming soon." Amen. Come Lord Jesus! (Rev 22:20).

However, the words of this final New Testament mystery still remain unfulfilled for us. And how soon is soon? After all, Jesus did tell us that only God, the Father, knows the exact moment (Mt 24: 36) and we are further told that to God 1000 years are as a day (Ps 90:4; 2 Ptr 3:8).[4]

NOTES

1. MT 13:11, The *mystery* of God, Christ Col 2:2; The *mystery* of God's will EPH 1:9;The *mystery* of Christ EPH 3:4; The *mystery* of the gospel EPH 6:19; The *mystery* of the faith 1 TIM 3:9; The *mystery* of devotion 1 TIM 3:16;The hidden wisdom of God's *mystery* 1COR 2:7, New American Bible, St. Joseph Edition, Confraternity of Christian Doctrine, Board of Trustees/ National Conference of Catholic Bishops/ United States Catholic Conference, Administrative and Editorial Committee/Board (New York, NY: Catholic Book Publishing Co., 1970). See also Jerome Biblical Commentary, Raymond E. Brown, S.S., Joseph Fitzmeyer, S.J., Roland Murphy, O. Carm., ed., (Englewood Cliffs, NJ: Prentice Hall Publishing, 1968) Sec 42:26; 53:9, 140; 55:21; 57:21–22; 79:14, 20, 34, 153.

2. Richard McBrien, Catholicism, (New York, NY: HarperCollins Pub., 1994) pp. 59–60; 138; 163; 166; 411; 449; 493; 495; 499–518; 532–579; 607–611; 698–699; 835–946; 1056–1057; 1123–1157. See also Jerome Biblical Commentary, Raymond E. Brown, S.S., Joseph Fitzmeyer, S.J., Roland Murphy, O. Carm., ed., (Englewood Cliffs, NJ: Prentice Hall Pub., 1968) Sec 20:7, 16; 34:30; 43:88–99; 48:16; 49:31; 77:149–151; 78:108; 44:5778:102–107; 78:93–108.

3. Col 2:2–3; EPH 1:9; 1 COR 4: 11; Tim 3:9; 1 Cor 15:51; 1 Cor 2:1–10; Rom 11:25; 16:25; Eph 1:9–10; 3:4–5; 6:19; Col 1:26; 4:3, New American Bible, St. Joseph Edition, Confraternity of Christian Doctrine, Board of Trustees/ National Conference of Catholic Bishops/United States Catholic Conference, Administrative and Editorial Committee/Board (New York, NY: Catholic Book Publishing Co., 1970).

4. Jerome Biblical Commentary, Raymond E. Brown, S.S., Joseph Fitzmeyer, S.J., Roland Murphy, O. Carm., ed., (Englewood Cliffs, NJ: Prentice Hall Pub., 1968) Sec 20:24; 64:1–97.

Chapter Sixteen

The Mystery of Suffering

THE INNOCENT SUFFER

Jesus Christ suffered. This is an historical reality. It is also a reality that many people in the world have suffered and are suffering today as well. Why God allows innocent people to suffer is a mystery. On the one hand, this mystery could be minimized because of its unpleasantness to contemplate. On the other hand, the mystery could be exaggerated, so that one never moves from the reality of Jesus crucifixion and suffering, as well as other's suffering. If we don't, we don't see the triumph and exaltation of resurrection. We also wouldn't interiorize this suffering, and if we don't, we won't ever become "contemplatives in action."

Any contemplation and reflection on mystery must include contemplation and reflection on suffering. If it does not, it overlooks the countless millions of brothers and sisters in the world whose reality it is to suffer daily. It also does not portray God's reality accurately. God, not only experienced immense suffering in the earthly Jesus of Nazareth, but also still suffers in the Holy Spirit that is within others who suffer in their realities today.

We do not have the power to eliminate the world's suffering, but what we can eliminate is our own unconsciousness to the existence of suffering. Any theology of mystery becomes mere ideology without entering into solidarity with those who suffer in their reality. It also blocks the grace which allows us to experience the Christ of the New Testament in the Holy Spirit.

One who has written extensively on the mystery of suffering is theologian Edward Schillebeeckx, recently deceased. He sees suffering as an important aspect of human life. To Schillebeeckx, "A flight from suffering is a flight to the status quo (*Christ*, E. Schillebeeckx)."[1] What he is implying is that we either make a "preferential option for the poor and suffering," or we will have consciously made a "preferential option for the status quo."

The impact suffering makes comes not only from those who suffer physically. Their suffering transcends their own suffering and causes us to reflect on their suffering in the light of the suffering of Jesus Christ. If we do not, we persist in a distorted picture of reality and the mystery that is God remains hidden from us. Human suffering is a mystery, both for those who believe in God and for those who do not. Any suffering can be united with Christ's suffering. Suffering, when accepted and offered up in union with the passion of Christ, can be redemptive.

But, as Christians, we cannot attempt to simply say we understand the mystery of suffering because of its redemptive character. This would be tantamount to telling those who are suffering, "chin up, your suffering is redemptive; it's all in the mysterious plan of God." That is not consciousness or even unconsciousness; that would be unconscionable.

What we must do, as Christians, is to locate the origin of that suffering within ourselves and make a conscious effort to eliminate it. Evil in the world is indicative of evil within us. Sin in the world is indicative of sin within us. Suffering in the world has something to do with our own suffering. God does not will suffering. God only allows suffering and somehow providentially wills to ultimately have it work for good. God wills love and goodness which transforms suffering.

Jesus resurrection can be seen in light of it being a divine corrective for the existence of suffering and evil in the world. Within the mystery of suffering, part of the irony is the source of suffering. Christianity and salvation are never a private affair. Often the mysteries of God are not experienced directly, but are sacramental and mediated realities. The Word of God can be mediated through the Bible without a doubt, by our contemplating on the suffering and passion of our Lord. But, it can also be mediated sacramentally through the cries of those who are suffering today. After the resurrection the Lord did tell us: "I am with you always, even unto the end of the world (MT 28:20)."[2]

And in similar fashion, in his book, *Christ*, Schilleebeeckx ends the book with the following observation he makes in the form of a short poem.

> "Rejoice and do not be dismayed,
> For God to whom we pray,
> Is closer than our closest friend,
> And in our midst today." *(Christ, E. Schillebeeckx)*[3]

NOTES

1. Edward Schillebeeckx, Christ, The Experience of Jesus as Lord, (New York, NY: Seabury Press, 1980) p. 745.
2. MT 28:20, New American Bible, St. Joseph Edition, Confraternity of Christian Doctrine, Board of Trustees/National Conference of Catholic Bishops/United States Catholic Conference, Administrative and Editorial Committee/Board (New York, NY: Catholic Book Publishing Co., 1970).
3. Edward Schillebeeckx, Christ, The Experience of Jesus as Lord, (New York, NY: Seabury Press, 1980) p. 840.

Chapter Seventeen

Miracles Mystery

SIGNS, WORKS, WONDER, POWER

The word "miracle," *(L. Mirculum)* can be defined as "An extraordinary event which manifests the supernatural work of God in human history."[1] Miracles are mysterious, first of all, because they seem to temporarily suspend what we know as reality.

In the Bible, the word is usually translated from the Hebrew words *mopet (symbolic act)* or *ot (sign)*. Neither word used by itself ever refers to anything necessarily marvelous. In the Old Testament, when something extraordinary is implied, the word *nipla (marvelous)* is added.

The New Testament doesn't use the word "miracle." There are two other words used more frequently in the Greek where a miracle is implied, they are *simeon (sign)* and *teras (wonder)*. The former is used more frequently than the latter. When *sign* is used, the word signifies a miracle which is an unaccustomed and unexpected event which serves as a motive for credibility by manifesting the power of God. When it is Christ performing the sign, the spectators are led to believe in his person. (ex. JN 2,11).

The word *wonder*, when used, implies that the spectators are awestruck and it indicates the element of surprised astonishment or amazement. Other than these two words, occasionally other words are used in the Greek to indicate that a miracle has taken place. Sometimes the term *erga (works)* is used, or *dynamis (power)*. Here what is indicated is that the doer has the power or ability to get something done and achieve a desired result.[2]

There are two extreme views concerning miracles. The first is to simply accept them in a fundamentalist way as having happened exactly the way they are described in the Bible in a literal fashion every time. The other extreme is to reject them out of hand because they presume to disrupt the system of order and the inflexible laws of nature. When in reality, if the mystery of miracles could be simply explained by natural law, they wouldn't be miracles.

I would suggest that the best path is "the golden mean," or to "navigate between the shoals." By taking the middle path, one can continue to keep in perspective what is the key thing with any of the New or Old Testament miracles and that is to see the significance of the miracle.

Miracles in the Bible should not be viewed within a closed system governed by rigid natural laws. It is the interference with so-called natural law that is actually termed a miracle. The great Sumatran tsunami in the Indian ocean that occurred in December 2004 was one of the deadliest natural disasters on record. It killed over 200,000 people in eleven countries. In August of 2005, Hurricane Katrina swept through seven states in the U.S., affecting the lives of 15 million people. And in January of 2009, Capt. Chesley (Sully) Sullenberger amazingly kept 155 people alive by gliding an engineless airplane from high in the sky and floating it onto the Hudson River. And who can forget the miraculous rescue of the 33 Chilean miners from a mile beneath the earth in 2010. Famines, plagues, and devastating floods or earthquakes as well, can all be viewed as ordinary workings of nature (reality) and as divine intervention or visitation (mystery). The distinction between the natural and supernatural, reality and mystery, is often tenuous at best.

The Hebrews of the Old Covenant, in particular, saw the forces of nature to not only be controlled by Yahweh for his own use, but also to manifest the presence of Yahweh. In the Old Testament, the most significant miracles occur when Yahweh delivers God's people out of Egypt. The account of these miracles is described in the entire first half of the Book of Exodus.[3]

In the New Testament, miracles are linked with the imminent inbreaking of the Kingdom of God into history. They are performed primarily by Jesus Christ and occasionally by the early disciples. Here, miracles manifest as extraordinary healings, epiphanies, exorcisms, rescues, gifts, or exercising supernatural powers or provisions (such as raising the dead). There is seen to be dominion over nature, both in the world and over human nature as well.[4]

To see Yahweh mysteriously in control of nature in the Old Testament is to see Jesus in control of nature in the New Testament. Nature "obeys" (Gk *hypakouei*) God. The wonder of the miracle is due to the fact that its cause by God is hidden and mysterious. A natural effect is expected other than what actually takes place. The character of the miracle turns the ordinary course and laws of nature (reality) into the extraordinary (mystery).

Miracles, in effect, transcend nature or are above or outside of nature or what we consider as reality. In that they are mystery, they are supernatural. Our experience of them cannot even be called surreal; they are more "trans-real." But we cannot label them as unreal or unnatural.

Among other things, the Bible is a record of God's providence. In it we are told that beyond the sphere of nature or what we experience as reality, that there exists another realm of existence which is called the supernatural or mystery. This is a realm populated by spiritual beings and departed souls. Both worlds are under God's providential governance. The occurrence of miracles takes place within the circle of the providence of God. Its supreme ends are the glory of God and the ultimate good of humankind. As human beings, we are rendered to silence when we cannot explain something. Miracles are certainly something that cannot easily be explained as God is appealing to man to take notice of God's reality instead of man's own reality.

I believe that you cannot profess to be a Christian without believing minimally in at least one miracle; that being the miracle of the resurrection of Jesus Christ from the dead. All miracles, including those performed by Jesus, were a prelude to the supreme miracle of the resurrection of Jesus. The resurrection is an end-time reality beyond all miracles as signs. And certainly, resurrection cannot be viewed strictly within the confines of what we know as reality, rationality, or naturality. As Paul writes,

> But if Christ is preached as raised from the dead, how can some among you say there is no resurrection from the dead? If there is no resurrection of the dead, then neither has Christ been raised. And if Christ has not been raised, then empty too is our preaching; empty too, your faith (1Cor 15:12–14).[5]

The miracle of the resurrection of Jesus Christ from the dead is no less a miracle for Christians than were the miracles performed by Yahweh surrounding the ancient Hebrews departure from Egypt. Following the ten plagues, in the first Passover, God had the Israelites mark their doorposts with the blood of the lamb. This was done so that the angel of death would miraculously pass over and spare them. Yahweh then used Moses to perform the miracle of parting the Red Sea, enabling the Israelites to cross safely to the other side (EX ch 7–14).[6]

The resurrection refers to an event which took place on the other side of death and beyond space and time. Therefore in addition to being called transreal, it should also be termed as transhistorical because it transcends history. With the resurrection, Jesus enters into a new and transcendent reality; God's reality. In the resurrection, Jesus Christ has sealed us with the Holy Spirit and marked us by the shedding of his blood, the blood of the innocent, slain lamb. This was done so that at death, the angel of death will pass us by and we will be spared. In the resurrection, Jesus essentially parted the blood of the entire sea of humanity and crossed to the other side.

What is literal reality and what is analogical reality in the case of either miracle, as described in scripture, can get lost in the details. It remains of little consequence as they are shrouded in mystery. In the case of the resurrection, in particular, we have no witnesses to the reality of the resurrection event. We do have empty tomb stories and post-crucifixion appearance stories. But, what is of importance and is evident is that something occurred as a real event in history in both instances.

In any of the Old Testament miracles, such as the parting of the Red Sea, or any of the New Testament miracles such as the resurrection, we find commonality. We can get lost in the hidden hows and whys which are wrapped up in the details of the mystery of the two miracles. Or we can find the significance and relevance of the reality of both miracles. In both instances, there is the ancient and future reality of finding out that you "crossed safely to the other side."

All miracles are signs that we live somewhere between what has been the previous "already happened" and the soon to be "not yet happened." For Christians alive now we await the relevant personal experience. While in the meantime, we live today in a "real-ly mystery-ous" world.

NOTES

1. "Miracle." Merriam-Webster Dictionary, Henry B. Woolff, ed. (Springfield, MA G & C. Merriam Co., 1974).

2. Richard McBrien, Catholicism, (New York, NY: HarperCollins Publishing, 1994) pp. 339–342. See also Jerome Biblical Commentary, Raymond E. Brown, S.S., Joseph Fitzmeyer, S.J., Roland Murphy, O. Carm., ed., (Englewood Cliffs, NJ: Prentice Hall Publishing, 1968) Sec 78:109–130; 42:30–33; 43:55; 3:19; 77:59; 53:133.

3. EX ch. 1–24, New American Bible, St. Joseph Edition, Confraternity of Christian Doctrine, Board of Trustees/ National Conference of Catholic Bishops/United States Catholic Conference, Administrative and Editorial Committee/Board (New York, NY: Catholic Book Publishing Co., 1970).

4. Jerome Biblical Commentary, Raymond E. Brown, S.S., Joseph Fitzmeyer, S.J., Roland Murphy, O. Carm., ed., (Englewood Cliffs, NJ: Prentice Hall Publishing, 1968) Sec 78:109–129; 42:30–33; 43:55.

5. 1Cor 15:12–14, New American Bible, St. Joseph Edition, Confraternity of Christian Doctrine, Board of Trustees/ National Conference of Catholic Bishops/ United States Catholic Conference, Administrative and Editorial Committee/Board (New York, NY: Catholic Book Publishing Co., 1970).

6. EX ch 7–14, New American Bible, St. Joseph Edition, Confraternity of Christian Doctrine, Board of Trustees/ National Conference of Catholic Bishops/United States Catholic Conference, Administrative and Editorial Committee/Board (New York, NY: Catholic Book Publishing Co., 1970).

Chapter Eighteen

The Hidden Kingdom

GOD'S MYSTICAL PRESENCE

When the word "Kingdom" is used in scripture it signifies a state of things in which God is recognized as king and we realize his kingship. So, "Kingdom of God" and "Kingdom of Heaven" have a basic equivalency. Kingdom of Heaven appears to be in continuity with the more Jewish expression as seen in most of the gospel of Matthew. Where "Heaven" is used as a synonym for God, there is the understanding that full participation in the transcendent reality is reserved for heaven and for God. The immanent reality is reserved for Jesus in his earthly ministry.

The Kingdom represents the reality of God's transforming presence, first in the hearts of human beings both personally and individually, then secondarily and collectively in groups and in the world. It is, at one and the same time, both the process and the ultimate reality which lies at the end of time and history when the process is complete. It is both in the now and in the as yet to come. The Kingdom is bringing about the unification of all reality and mystery within history.

"Reign of God," when used in scripture, can be seen in somewhat different terms. It is the more active and dynamic expression for the rule of God in the Kingdom. It is the Kingdom in the process of being "realized." The message of the "Reign/Kingdom of God" is the central element in the entire preaching of Jesus. It becomes for us who live in the present, more an acceptance of the royal power, sovereignty, and dignity of God as our reality (Reign), and only secondarily to be considered as a realm (Kingdom).[1]

The Old Testament uses the term "Kingdom of God" only once in the *Book of Wisdom* (Wis 10:10), however, the kingship of Yahweh permeates all of the Old Testament books. The Kingdom, as a present/future reality is particularly evident in the writings of the prophets.[2]

The Kingdom was more of a reality than a profound mystery for Jesus. He was convinced that the Reign of God was active and being realized in his preaching, his works, and his very person. Jesus did not simply proclaim the Kingdom of God as a reality, he practiced it in reality. He saw himself as being related to the earthly manifestation of the divine reality of the Kingdom.

Jesus never really defined the Kingdom, he used the term primarily in parables (MK 4:30–34). However, we do know that he saw it as very inclusive, and many of the people it was open to were some of the most unlikely participants. They were the poor, oppressed, tax collectors, prostitutes, sinners, meek, despised, and the sick and infirm.

But what really surprised Jesus hearers of the Gospel was his depiction of the Kingdom as an imminent reality. For example, Jesus proclaimed that the Kingdom is "in your midst (LK 17:21)," that it had, "come near (MK 1:15)," was "at hand (MT 4:17)," and had, "overtaken you (MT 12:28)."[3]

It is for us that the Kingdom is more of a mystery than a reality. But, our individual realities are not separate from the reality of the Kingdom. God is "realizing" the Kingdom in our loving relationships with one another every day, even though we may not "realize" what is taking place. For us, it remains mostly a mystery. Although a mystery, it is not a power outside of ourselves, but one placed in our hearts by the presence of God dwelling there. God is being one with us in our reality. While at the same time, God is one with us in our reality, God is simultaneously reconciling, renewing, and unifying. God is bringing everything (including us) into the oneness of his love and out of our mystery into his reality.

After all, there is only one origin or beginning, and ultimately only one end for all that exists as created reality, and that is God, the reality. God is the destiny and the consummation of all that exists. That this will indeed happen is no mystery. The only mystery associated with it is how this all happens for us. That part remains hidden with the one who holds the keys to the hidden Kingdom. For even Jesus said that God alone knows the hour of its final coming: "That day and hour no one knows, neither the angels of heaven, nor the son, but the Father alone (Mt 24:36)."[4]

The hidden kingdom is not something totally in the future. It is coming to be in the ongoing history of the world in active love. We live now, somewhere "between the times"—between the consummation of Kingdom mystery and the fullness of experiencing Kingdom reality.

NOTES

1. Richard McBrien, Catholicism, (New York, NY: HarperCollins Publishing, 1994) pp. 59–60; 500–579; 607–699; 891–908. See also Jerome Biblical Commentary, Raymond E. Brown, S.S., Joseph Fitzmeyer, S.J., Roland Murphy, O. Carm., ed., (Englewood Cliffs, NJ: Prentice Hall Publishing, 1968) Sec 20:7–16; 42: 12–44:125; 55:14–56; 78:96–107.

2. Wis 10:10, New American Bible, St. Joseph Edition, Confraternity of Christian Doctrine, Board of Trustees/National Conference of Catholic Bishops/United States Catholic Conference, Administrative and Editorial Committee/Board (New York, NY: Catholic Book Publishing Co., 1970).

3. MK 4:30–34; LK 17:21; MK 1:15; MT 12:28, New American Bible, St. Joseph Edition, Confraternity of Christian Doctrine, Board of Trustees/ National Conference of Catholic Bishops/United States Catholic Conference, Administrative and Editorial Committee/Board (New York, NY: Catholic Book Publishing Co., 1970).

4. Mt 24:36, New American Bible, St. Joseph Edition, Confraternity of Christian Doctrine, Board of Trustees/ National Conference of Catholic Bishops/United States Catholic Conference, Administrative and Editorial Committee/Board (New York, NY: Catholic Book Publishing Co., 1970).

Chapter Nineteen

Those Peculiar Parables

A MYSTERIOUS LANGUAGE

"I will open my mouth in parables, I will utter mysteries of old (Ps 78:2; Mt 13:35)."
That the coming Messiah would open his mouth and speak in parables, the mysterious language of the Wisdom writers, is first prophesied in the Old Testament book of Psalms (Ps 78:2). That Jesus would speak in this parabolic language would then be confirmed in the New Testament in Matthew's gospel (Mt 13:35).[1]
When something is called "hidden," it indicates its mysterious character, as well as the difficulty one might encounter in grasping the reality. Finding the "hidden Kingdom" is similar to finding the "Magic Kingdom." If you want to find the hidden Kingdom, you would first go to the Bible. If you want to find the Magic Kingdom, you would first go to Disneyworld. In either case, once there, you would then need to follow the signs to find it.
Jesus accompanied his words with many mighty signs or "works." He himself, of course, is the most significant sign of the Kingdom. The Kingdom is within him (Lk 7:18–23; Acts 2:22). The miracles also did attest that the Father had sent him as the Son of God, so they are signs as well (JN 10:31–38). The miracles became not only signs that brought faith in Jesus; they also became occasions for offense (MT 11:6). After all, the miracles were not signs Jesus worked to satisfy people's curiosity for magic. They even brought accusations that Jesus was acting by demonic power (MK 3:21).
So, there is yet another sign that Jesus used to point the way to the Kingdom. This sign for the hidden Kingdom is the parable. Jesus usually spoke about the Kingdom in a parable (MT 13:31; MK 4:34; LK 8:4). The parable was a method Jesus used to reveal the mystery of the Kingdom to his disciples. While

at the same time, the meaning and intent of the reality of the Kingdom would be heard, but would remain hidden from the understanding of others. Jesus would say, "Knowledge of the mysteries of the Kingdom of God has been granted to you, but to the rest they are made known through parables so that they may look but not see, and hear but not understand (MK 4:11; Lk 8:10)."[2]

The fundamental element in a parable is the element of metaphor. A metaphor is a figure of speech in which words or phrases literally denoting certain kinds of objects, ideas, or realities are used in place of others to suggest likeness or analogies between them. Jesus spoke about the Kingdom, which was a hidden and unknown reality using things which were illustrations from the reality of daily life. These included seeds, weeds, wheat, yeast, treasure, pearls, nets, fish, etc. All of these were commonly known (MT 13).

There would be in every parable an evident reality along with the hidden mystery which was the Kingdom. It wasn't Jesus intention, it seems, to hide the Kingdom from some, but that was just the result of the preaching. The great majority, then as now, see and hear the parables of the Kingdom, but refuse to perceive and understand the reality. The challenge for all disciples, then as now, is the same. It is to see the reality of the Kingdom through reflection and contemplation on the parabolic mysteries. The parables continue to reveal more and more hidden meaning.[3]

NOTES

1. Ps 78:2; Mt 13:35; Ps 78:2; Mt 13:35, New American Bible, St. Joseph Edition, Confraternity of Christian Doctrine, Board of Trustees/ National Conference of Catholic Bishops/United States Catholic Conference, Administrative and Editorial Committee/Board (New York, NY: Catholic Book Publishing Co., 1970).

2. Lk 7:18–23; Acts 2:22; JN 10:31–38; MT 11:6; MK 3:21; MT 13:31; MK 4:34; LK 8:4; MK 4:11; Lk 8:10, New American Bible, St. Joseph Edition, Confraternity of Christian Doctrine, Board of Trustees/National Conference of Catholic Bishops/ United States Catholic Conference, Administrative and Editorial Committee/Board (New York, NY: Catholic Book Publishing Co., 1970).

3. Jerome Biblical Commentary, Raymond E. Brown, S.S., Joseph Fitzmeyer, S.J., Roland Murphy, O. Carm., ed., (Englewood Cliffs, NJ: Prentice Hall Publishing, 1968) Sec. 78:100–145 See also MT 13, New American Bible, St. Joseph Edition, Confraternity of Christian Doctrine, Board of Trustees/ National Conference of Catholic Bishops/United States Catholic Conference, Administrative and Editorial Committee/Board (New York, NY: Catholic Book Publishing Co., 1970).

Chapter Twenty

Mysticism

MYSTERY AS THEOLOGY

As was stated earlier, long ago theology was defined by Anselm in the early church as "faith seeking understanding."[1] That is still, perhaps, the most acceptable definition today for all of theology. When one seeks to understand mystery as theology, however, this does not work as an acceptable definition. The starting point here must be the recognition that you will probably end up with more faith and a lot less in the way of understanding. You will end up with bigger questions than you had previously and not so many concrete answers. You yourself, will end up not only as the questioner, but also as the one being questioned.

"Mysticism" can be called, the process by which our consciousness and understanding is transformed, so that we are enabled, through grace, to experience God more deeply. We experience God both as a Divine mystery and an invisible reality. The process ultimately leads to a deeper union with God as ultimate reality.[2]

Mysticism is also a spiritual and bodily experience of mystery as transcendent reality. At God's initiative as Holy Spirit, the spirit within the human person is given a direct experience of God through the movement of grace.

In a theological sense, the etymology of the word "mystery" has come to mean "religious truth via Divine Revelation." The use of the word mystery in this manner signals the mystical presence of the hidden God. In conformity with the usage of the inspired writers of both the Old and New Testaments, theologians give the name mystery to the truths of revelation that surpass the powers of the natural reason of our humanity. Mystery then, in its strict theological sense, is in no way synonymous with the incomprehensible. All that we know is incomprehensible; that is, it is not adequately comprehensible with the unknowable. Many things merely natural are accidentally unknowable on account of their inaccessibility. For example, things that are future, remote, or hidden are naturally unknowable and inaccessible. In its strict sense then, a mystery is a supernatural truth, one that by its very nature lies above or transcends the finite intelligence, logic, and reason of our humanity and can only be revealed by God. through mystical experience.[3]

At the heart of all mysticism lies a belief that essentially all reality is oneness or exists in union with a transcendant God. The universe which contains countless millions of persons, stars, animals, galaxies, plant life, and all else has a oneness. Any separation of these is not reality, but an illusion. Therefore, reality can only be truly known through one's spiritual experience of mystery or mysticism.

There is what is called the "Hermeneutic Circle." The name originated with the Greek God Hermes, who was the interpreter and messenger of the Gods. When applied to Christian Mystical Theology, it applies to the balancing and interpreting of the experiences of God. It can be imagined as a three-legged stool. Doing theology as mystery should always be balanced between the experience of the mystery of God in us, the experience of the mystery of God in others (Traditionally and particularly Christians, past and present), and the experience of the mystery of God contained in the Bible as the Word of God. It should have a communal basis.[4]

Even for mystics, monastics, and hermits, the Christian life has always been lived in communion with the community of believers, which is the Christian church on earth. It is always advisable to participate in corporate worship and to also have a spiritual director, mentor, or minimally, at least a "soul friend." This should be someone with whom we can discuss our spiritual progress. We should always have people around us who, in the face of the deepest mysteries of God, will at times just simply tell us to "GET REAL."

Mystery is sacramental in nature and can be experienced as a mediation of reality through the scriptures, nature, another person, or any other part of the created world where there is openness to the power of God to self-communicate the spiritual dimension of reality. The greatest proof of Divine and unconditional love is the gift of a perfect self. Goodness by its very nature is self-diffusive. Thomas Aquinas has said, "It belongs to the essence of goodness to communicate itself to others."[5]

So, Christians are called to be first "Temples of the Holy Spirit (1 COR 6:19);" then to bear the "Fruit of the Spirit: love, joy, peace, patience, kindness, gentleness, faithfulness, humility, and self-control (GAL 5:22)," to others, as facets of this love and dimensions of this goodness in us.

Christian theology generally maintains that God dwells in all Christians through the power of the Holy Spirit and that Christians can experience

God through belief in Jesus Christ. Christian mysticism, therefore, aspires to apprehend spiritual and theological truths inaccessible through intellectual means or reason. This is experienced as mystery within the totality of our humanity, typically by putting on the mind of Christ. Galatians 2: 19–20 states, for example, "I have been crucified with Christ; yet I live no longer I; but Christ lives in me . . ."

This mystery is further confirmed when Paul speaks about it again in Colossians 1: 26–27, when he says, "God chose to make known the riches of the glory of this mystery among the Gentiles; it is Christ in you, the hope for glory."[6]

Christian mysticism implies that one should be seeking a complete identification with Christ and that through the grace of God and the power of the Holy Spirit one is living their life in imitation of Christ. In doing this, God is able to begin to achieve a unification of the human spirit with the Spirit of God, the Holy Spirit. This same experience of Christ crucified in us was also spoken about by many of the early church fathers, particularly Clement of Alexandria and Origen.[7]

We know through a reading of the New Testament that others have had experiences of Christian mysticism. Certainly, the Apostle Paul seems to indicate that there were experiences that were beyond the intellectual, logical, and power of human reason. For example, in 2 Corinthians 12:2–4, Paul speaks about a possible out-of-body experience by someone who was taken up to the "third heaven," and taught unutterable mysteries. Here he states that, "This person (whether in the body or out of the body, I do not know, God knows) was caught up into Paradise and heard ineffable things, which no one may utter."[8]

For Christians who seek the experience of theology as mystery, there must take place a gradual transformation of the spiritual self. This will begin with the seeking of unification with the Holy Spirit in prayerful reflection and contemplation. Then by harmonious communion with God and desiring to become a "contemplative in action," there will commence the habitual daily practice of virtue (the power to do good) and the modification, reduction, or elimination of vice.

This will place one on a path to become a more fully "realized" human person created in the image and likeness of God. For Christians, this human potential has been realized most perfectly in Jesus, because he is both God and human. But, this potential can also be mysteriously manifested in others, both consciously and unconsciously through their mystical association with Jesus in the Holy Spirit.

Particularly when meditating on the word of God in the scriptures, the soul can be illuminated by the light of the Holy Spirit. The Holy Spirit will begin to enlighten the mind, giving mysterious insights into truths not only explicit in scripture and in the Christian traditions, but also through illuminating many of the deeper aspects of reality. The God of Mystery will begin to be experienced through all of reality. God will, essentially GET REAL for us. One will begin to see and experience "signals of transcendence" in everyone and everything. Christian mysticism is a call for all Christians to enter into the Divine Mystery of God. Tielhard de Chardin has said, "The entire universe is one Divine Mileau *(Divine Mileau, T. De Chardin)*."[9]

Ultimately, one will experience the mysterious reality of being forever united with God. We will realize ourselves to be both a human being and a human becoming. This mystical union will allow for having an experience of both unconditional and divine Love, as well as perfect Goodness. This does not imply, of course, that we will be either Divine or Perfect; only that we will have been given the power to change and be transformed. Only God IS Love and only God IS Good, both by essence and existence. For each of us, however, who seek to practice theology as mystery, it is the journey which IS the goal.

NOTES

1. Anselm, Theistic Proofs, Proslogion, 2:1. Found in Edward N. Zalta, ed., Stanford Encyclopedia of Philosophy (Stanford, CA: Stanford Center For The Study of Language and Information, Stanford University, 2008 Edition). Found on the Standford University Encyclopedia of Philosophy website at http://plato.stanford.edu/entries/anselm/#FaiSeeUndChaPurAnsThePro (accessed 10/10/2009). See also "Glossary/Theology" in Richard P. McBrien, ed., Catholicism: New Study Edition (New York, NY: HarperCollins Publishers, 1994) p. 1258.

2. "Mysticism." Encyclopedia of Theology, The Concise Sacramentum Mundi, Karl Rahner ed., (New York, NY: Seabury/Crossroads Press, 1975) pp. 1004–1111. See also Jerome Biblical Commentary, Raymond E. Brown, S.S., Joseph Fitzmeyer, S.J., Roland Murphy, O. Carm., ed., (Englewood Cliffs, NJ: Prentice Hall Publishing, 1968) Sec. 53:9, 140; 57:21–22.

3. Jerome Biblical Commentary, Raymond E. Brown, S.S., Joseph Fitzmeyer, S.J., Roland Murphy, O. Carm., ed., (Englewood Cliffs, NJ: Prentice Hall Publishing, 1968) Sec 53:9, 140; 57:21–22; 55:21; 79:14, 20, 34, 153; 48:33; 51:18; 79:11, 32–34; 56:6, 14–15, 19, 38; 41:40–41. See also Richard McBrien, Catholicism, (New York, NY: HarperCollins Publishing, 1994) pp. 207–217; 232–234; 351; 597;1063–1067; 1085–1086; 1181. And Encyclopedia of Theology, The Concise Sacramentum Mundi, Karl Rahner ed., (New York, NY: Seabury/Crossroads Press, 1975) pp. 1000–1004.

4. "Hermeneutics." Catholic Encyclopedia, From the New Advent Encyclopedia, found on the New Advent CD-ROM by Kevin Knight (Denver, CO: Advent Inter-

national, 2009). See also the New Advent website at http://www.newadvent.org/cathen/07271a.htm.

5. Thomas Aquinas, Summa Theologica, Question 1, Articles 1–6, found on the New Advent CD-ROM by Kevin Knight (Denver, CO: Advent International, 2009). See also the New Advent website at http://www.newadvent.org/summa/4001.htm.

6. 1 COR 6:19; GAL 5:22; Gal 2: 19–20; Col 1: 26–27, New American Bible, St. Joseph Edition, Confraternity of Christian Doctrine, Board of Trustees/National Conference of Catholic Bishops/United States Catholic Conference, Administrative and Editorial Committee/Board (New York, NY: Catholic Book Publishing Co., 1970).

7. Clement of Alexandria, The Stromata, Church Fathers, found on the New Advent CD-ROM by Kevin Knight (Denver, CO: Advent International, 2009). See also the New Advent website at http://www.newadvent.org/fathers/02101.htm See also Origen, Commentary on Matthew, Book xxii, New Advent website at http://www.newadvent.org/fathers/101612.htm.

8. 2 Cor 12:2–4, New American Bible, St. Joseph Edition, Confraternity of Christian Doctrine, Board of Trustees/ National Conference of Catholic Bishops/United States Catholic Conference, Administrative and Editorial Committee/Board (New York, NY: Catholic Book Publishing Co., 1970).

9. Teilhard de Chardin, Divine Mileau, (New York, NY: HarperCollins Publishing, 1960) p. 97.

Chapter Twenty-One

Two Types of Theological Mysteries

ABSOLUTE AND RELATIVE MYSTERIES

Theologians distinguish between two types of supernatural truths as mysteries: The first is the absolute mystery. An absolute mystery is a supernatural truth whose existence or possibility could not be discovered by a human being. Although it has been revealed, the essence of an absolute mystery (its inner substantial being) can only be expressed by the finite human mind in terms of analogy, e.g., the Trinity.[1]

Secondly, there is the relative mystery. A relative mystery is a supernatural truth whose innermost nature alone and essence (e.g., many of the Divine attributes), or whose existence alone exceeds the natural knowing power of the creature. It lies beyond the human capacity for thought and cannot be found through reason or logic alone.[2]

These two types of mysteries are not simply disconnected supernatural truths lying beyond the realm of natural things, but a higher, heavenly world, in a mystical universe whose parts are united in a living bond and in beautiful and glorious harmony. In this mystical universe, although hidden, and to a great extent humanly unknowable, there is no war between revelation and reason. In this mystical universe, there lies more unconditional love, perfect goodness, supernatural truth, unknown reality, and unrevealed mystery.

AN ABSOLUTE MYSTERY-TRIUNITY

I will not be saying too much about the Trinity, as it is a revealed mystery which I don't pretend to fully comprehend. God is a mysterious ultimate reality whose existence can neither be proven, nor disproved by human beings. To paraphrase Augustine, "For those who do not believe, no proof will ever be enough; for those who believe, no proof is necessary."³

The Trinity is an absolute mystery. This implies that even though it has been revealed, we still cannot fully understand it or comprehend it. The mystery transcends the human imagination and capacity for rational and logical thinking. Even if we think we understand it, we don't.

Human persons often attempt to develop any understanding of transcendent reality, through analogy. For example, one of the most frequently utilized analogies for the Trinity is water. Liquid water is water, steam is water, and ice is water. Another common analogy is the shamrock. Analogy is an important dimension of our rational and logical thought process in this regard. With the absolute mystery of the Trinity this will never work too well for us because analogy is based on the principle of comparative similarity. Here the dissimilarities will always be greater in making any analogy of the Trinity. Any analogy made between God's transcendent reality and man's human reality will always end up being totally inadequate.

The Christian church has always used the terms "person" or "hypostasis" to designate the Father, Son, and Holy Spirit as a real distinction of three persons in the one Godhead. The term "relation" is used to designate the fact that their distinction lies in relationship to the others. But, as Christians, we do not confess three Gods, we confess one God in three distinct persons.

While they are called three persons in view of their distinctions and their relations, we believe that they are one nature or substance; they are conatural and consubstantial. Because of their "Trinity," the Father is wholly in the Son and the Holy Spirit; the Holy Spirit is wholly in the Father and in the Son. We can experience the Holy Spirit sent by the Father and/through the Son as it proceeds. Can there be more of a mystery than the Trinity?⁴

The word, "Trinity" is never mentioned in the Bible. But, for that matter, neither is the word "Bible" mentioned in the Bible. It's only stated on the cover. In Romans 8:9–11, Paul will use the terms "Spirit of God," Spirit of Christ," and "Spirit of Him who raised Jesus from the dead," interchangeably in his description of the indwelling of God in the Christian. Matthew, the gospel writer, will also tell us, "Go and teach all nations, baptizing them in the name of the Father, and of the Son, and of the Holy Ghost" (Mt 28:18). This scriptural passage certainly describes three distinct persons in the unity of one Godhead.

The word, "Trinity," itself to describe the transcendent reality of God and the mysterious unity of the Godhead has been in use since the first few centuries of the Christian church. Some of the other scriptural references which laid the groundwork for the ensuing later development of the doctrine of the Trinity within the Christian churches were Jn 1:1–34; Rom 5:1–5, 8:14–17, 15:30; 2Cor 1:21–22, 13:13; 1Cor 2:7–16, 6:11, 12:4–6.[5]

In the Mystery of the Holy Trinity, God calls us to intimate union with The Father, Son, and Holy Spirit while we are living somewhere between the tension of the already and the not-yet. It remains as an experience of mystery which can be humanly experienced but not fully or consciously "realized." The Trinity is the ultimate reality of God and the ultimate mystery of man.

NOTES

1. From the Dogmatic Constitution on the Catholic Faith, Vatican I, 1870. See Richard McBrien, Catholicism, (New York, NY: HarperCollins Publishing, 1994) p. 316. See also "The Trinity." Karl Rahner, Encyclopedia of Theology, The Concise Sacramentum Mundi, Karl Rahner ed., (New York, NY: Seabury/Crossroads Press, 1975) pp. 1755–1771.

2. "Relative Mystery." Catholic Encyclopedia, From the New Advent Encyclopedia, found on the New Advent CD-ROM by Kevin Knight (Denver, CO: Advent International, 2009). See also the New Advent website at http://www.newadvent.org/cathen/10662a.htm.

3. Augustine, Confessions, Confessions and Letters of Augustine, Phillip Schaaf, ed. (New York, NY: Schaaf Church Publishing, 1884) Found online at Googlebooks.com. See Googlebooks at http://books.google.com/books?id=qbwPBnMK05kC&printsec=frontcover#v=onepage&q&f=false.

4. "The Trinity." Karl Rahner, Encyclopedia of Theology, The Concise Sacramentum Mundi, Karl Rahner ed., (New York, NY: Seabury/Crossroads Press, 1975) pp. 1755–1771.

5. Rom 8:9–11; Mt 28:18; Jn 1:1–34; Rom 5:1–5, 8:14–17, 15:30; 2Cor 1:21–22, 13:13; 1Cor 2:7–16, 6:11, 12:4–6, New American Bible, St. Joseph Edition, Conf. of Christian Doctrine, Board of Trustees/ National Conf. of Catholic Bishops/United States Catholic Conf., Adm. and Editorial Committee/Board (New York, NY: Catholic Book Publishing Co., 1970).

Chapter Twenty-Two

The Mystery of the Female

A UNITY OF TWO

Being male and female is a reality willed by God in God's image.[1] It is a unity of two. But God is not in man's image and is neither male nor female. As a male, who has never had the full personal, earthly life experience of the female; the female is, first of all, mysterious to me by nature. I have not had the direct experience of being a female; therefore, I can never fully comprehend that experience here on earth. For me, it is a mediated reality. Any knowledge I have about the female can only come from education, observation, communication, and interaction. The closest I have ever come to the experience of being in unity with a female in this earthly life is to have been happily married for over 45 years. In that sense, my wife, Terri, and I are a unity of two. However, her female experience is still direct and mine is a mediated reality.

THE SECRET OF LIFE

Every woman has the potential to carry within herself a sacred secret which is most mysterious. This secret is life. The name *Eve* in the Hebrew is *Hawwa* and is related to the Hebrew word *hay* which means "living." Therefore the name *Eve* is translated from the Hebrew to mean "the mother of the living."[2]

In the mystery which is the female body, human life finds its beginning: not in the male semen but in the fertilized egg, hidden in the deep recesses of the female body. It is there that God creates a new soul which is exclusively his handiwork. At this point, neither father nor mother has a part. The female does not consciously know how to bring the life of a soul into her womb and help it to form a spirited body. And yet this profound mystery which is the reality of life, takes place within her unknowingly; by this I mean without her full "realization."

This new creation takes place after the male seed fertilizes the female egg. Thus at that very moment that the egg is fertilized, a closeness exists between the divine action shrouded in mystery and the reality of the female body. Out of the substance of the female's very being, life comes forth. She participates and cooperates with divine action in the great mystery of bringing a soul into life. She is also part of the divine mystery of spirit being born into matter. To me, this marks the female body as mysterious sacred ground.

The sacredness of life is a mystery not written down in any book. It belongs to the heartbeat, the rhythm of breath, and the flow from blood to blood, within the female. It can only be directly experienced by the female. The feminine is the mysterious interconnectedness of all of life in a way that is veiled from the male.

Everything is part of the whole in the circle of life. But, only the female knows this oneness through direct experience. She probably senses it in the deep recesses of her body through her instinctual wisdom. However, the femininity of wisdom is slowly giving rise to a male consciousness as well, in order to communicate in the voice of the male. Males hear the music playing very often, but it is only the lady who knows how to dance to the rhythm of creation.

A RADIANT LIFE

by Michael Hickey

Circles encircled,
The many into one;
A universe personalized,
In eyeing the sun.

Alpha and omega,
Beginning without end;
Living life on the periphery;
Centered only when we bend.

Cycles of days,
Rounds out tomorrow;
Providential wheel of fortune;
Joy circumscribes sorrow.

Revolving through years,
Planets orbit the sun,
Blood's circulating pattern,
Beats hearts of everyone.

Global people connected,
Each life affects another;
Moon, Menstrual cycles, ovulation;
Woman evolves into mother.

Will we ever be whole;
Integrated as we grow?
"'Round comes 'round"
We reap what we sow.

NOTES

1. Gen 1:27; New American Bible, St. Joseph Edition, Confraternity of Christian Doctrine, Board of Trustees/National Conference of Catholic Bishops/United States Catholic Conference, Administrative and Editorial Committee/Board (New York, NY: Catholic Book Publishing Co., 1970).

2. Jerome Biblical Commentary, Raymond E. Brown, S.S., Joseph Fitzmeyer, S.J., Roland Murphy, O. Carm., ed., (Englewood Cliffs, NJ: Prentice Hall Publishing, 1968) Sec. 2: 22–29.

Chapter Twenty-Three

A Beginning and End Times Mystery

MICHAEL?

The name, "Michael," has been corrupted in modern times to render its meaning as "godlike" or "who is like God." Several books on the etymology of names give this as a definition of the name, but I believe they are in error. Because it is my own first name, given to me at birth by my parents, I have always been curious about the meaning of the name. In fact, I had an intense debate about the meaning of the name with a Catholic priest several years ago. He insisted that the above etymologies were correct and I insisted that he was not accurate.

The name is derived from the ancient Hebrew name (Mikha'el). As was discussed earlier, names were very important to the ancient Hebrew and great significance was attached to personal names. They revealed character and identity indicated who the person was and how they conducted themselves.[1] In Hebrew thought, "to know Mikha'el," is "to encounter the personal reality who is Mikha'el." But, a person cannot be known unless their name is known. As was also stated previously, in the Hebrew language there is an association between the person and the name which is unlike our language. Where the Hebrew language might use the word "name," we might use "person" or "self." To "know" the name is to then "know" the reality named. This is why it is important to translate the name properly.[2]

The great majority of the books on the etymology of names do render the meaning of the name "Michael" correctly. Its intended meaning as translated from the Hebrew name "Mikha'el" is "Who is like God?" Note the question mark. The connotation is not a statement. It is a rhetorical question, implying no person is like God. To know the reality named as "Michael," would be to know that there is no-one like God.[3]

THE ARCHANGEL AND SCRIPTURE

Michael is considered an archangel in the Jewish, Christian, and Islamic traditions. An archangel is considered to be an angel of high rank. The word "angel" (*L. Angelus*) is translated from the Hebrew as "messenger." Angels are represented throughout the Bible as a created body of spiritual beings, intermediate between God and humanity.[4]

In origin, Michael was one of the seven archangels in Hebrew tradition and the only one identified as an archangel in the Bible. Michael is a principal angel; his name (Who is like God?) was the war-cry of the good angels in the battle fought in heaven against the enemy and his followers at the beginning of time. The name is referenced four times in Scripture:

(1) In the Old Testament book of Daniel (DN 10:13–22), Gabriel says to Daniel, when he asks God to permit the Jews to return to Jerusalem: "The prince of the kingdom of Persia resisted me . . . and, finally Michael, one of the chief princes, came to help me . . . No one supports me against all these, but Michael your prince . . ."

(2) In Daniel 12:1, the Angel speaking of the end of the world and the Antichrist says: "At that time there shall arise Michael, the great prince, guardian of your people; . . ."

The Old Testament book of Daniel is the only specific reference to the archangel Michael by name in the entire Old Testament. There is a veiled reference in the book of Joshua which is believed to refer to Michael. Here Joshua is near Jericho and encounters an angel with a sword in his hand. When Joshua asks whether friend or foe, he is told by the angel that his identity is "The commander of the host of the Lord (JO 5:13–15)."

(3) In the New Testament Epistle of St. Jude (JD 1:9) it is written: "Yet the archangel Michael when he argued with the devil, in a dispute over the body of Moses, did not venture to pronounce a reviling judgement upon him but said, 'May the Lord rebuke you!'"

Jude is alluding to an ancient Hebrew tradition concerning a dispute between Michael and Satan over the body of Moses. There is no other account of this in either the Old or New Testaments. Although, there could be a veiled reference to this in 2 PTR 2: 10–11. The Old Testament account of the death and burial of Moses in Deuteronomy only states that Moses died in the land of Moab and was buried in a ravine across from Beth-peor. It further states that "to this day no one knows the place of his burial (DT 34:6)." This account that the writer of Jude is referencing in verse 9 appears to be something discussed in an apocryphal book, *The Assumption of Moses*. This is confirmed by the early church father, Origen (*Origen, De Principiis III.2.2*).

Here, God dispatches Michael to bury the body of Moses; Satan, however, wishes to lay claim to it on the grounds of its materiality.

(4) In the book of Revelation (RV 12:7), the writer John says "Then war broke out in heaven; Michael and his angels battled against the dragon . . ."[5]

Satan is the accuser of God's people and Michael the defender. John is speaking of the great conflict at the end of time, which also reflects the battle in heaven at the beginning of time. The Messiah's exaltation is linked with Michael's victory. Michael's triumph is made possible because of the enthronement of the lamb. The victory doesn't really belong to Michael, but to God. Michael is not just an angel and the leader of the heavenly host, he is first and foremost, God's servant.

According to the early Church Fathers, there are also questions concerning the veiled presence of Michael in Scripture where his name is not mentioned. They say he was the cherub who stood at the gate of paradise, "to keep the way of the tree of life(GN 3:24)," the angel through whom God published the Decalogue to his chosen people, the angel who stood in the way against Balaam (Numbers 22:22), and the angel who routed the army of Sennacherib (2 Kings 19:35).[6]

THE ARCHANGEL AND CHRISTIAN TRADITION

Following these Scriptural passages, Christian tradition gives to Michael these offices:

1. Fight against Satan.
2. Rescue the souls of the faithful from the power of the enemy.
3. Be a champion of God's people (Jews under the Old Law, Christians in the New Testament).
4. At the time of death to accompany the dead into the presence of God for judgement.[7]

THE ARCHANGEL AND APOCRYPHA

Outside of scriptural sources, Michael is mentioned in many of the Hebrew and Christian apocryphal writings in addition to *The Assumption of Moses*. The oldest known Hebrew work not included in the Bible is *The Book of Enoch*. It was assumed to have been written in the Third or Fourth Century BC. Ten Enoch manuscripts were discovered among *The Dead Sea Scrolls* at Qumran in 1947.

Enoch opens by telling the reader that it is a book written for a remote generation yet to come. Michael is described as the holy angel who is "set over the best part of mankind and over chaos (EN 20)." He is further mentioned as "the leader of the angels (EN 24)." He guards the Tree of Life and issues a warning not to touch it (EN 25).[8]

Another example of Hebrew apocrypha where Michael is mentioned is *The War of the Sons of Light against the Sons of Darkness*. Here Michael is described as the Prince of Light leading the forces of God against the darkness of evil. He is depicted as "The Viceroy of Heaven."[9]

In Christian apocrypha, perhaps the most notable is a Second Century piece titled *The Shepard of Hermas*. This book was actually considered as canonical in the early church. Many of the early Church Fathers reference it as Canonical Scripture. These would include Ireneus and Tertullian. The book describes Michael as "a great and glorious angel who has authority over his people and governs them (SH BK III, SIM 8, CH 3)."[10]

He is also described as the guardian of Paradise and the bodies of Adam and Eve in the Ante-Nicene fathers apocryphal writing *The Revelation of Moses*. Here is an excerpt:

> The Lord of the universe, sitting upon His holy throne, stretched forth His hands, and raised Adam, and delivered him to the archangel Michael, saying to him: Raise him into paradise, even to the third heaven, and let him be there until that great and dreadful day which I am to bring upon the world. And the archangel Michael, having taken Adam, led him away, and anointed him, as God said to him at the pardoning of Adam. After all these things, therefore, the archangel asked about the funeral rites of the remains; and God commanded that all the angels should come together into His presence, each according to his rank. And all the angels were assembled, some with censers, some with trumpets. And the Lord of Hosts went up, and the winds drew Him, and cherubim riding upon the winds, and the angels of heaven went before Him; and they came to where the body of Adam was, and took it (*NT Apoc. Vol. VIII*).[11]

Many of the Christian Fathers of the early church in their writings describe Michael as the leader of the heavenly host. These would include many of the Greek Fathers, as well as Origen, Basil the Great, Bellarmine, Bonaventure, and Pseudo-Dionysius.[12]

Outside of Judaism and Christianity, Islam, in the Qur'an, mentions Michael only once as a good angel (Sura 2:98).[13] Both Seventh Day Adventists and Jehovah's Witnesses believe that Jesus and the Archangel Michael are one and the same being.[14] Mormons believe that the Archangel Michael and Adam are one and the same being. There is no basis to substantiate either assumption which can be found conclusively in either Scripture or the broader Judeo-Christian traditions.

A MYSTERIOUS END-TIMES ROLE

One of Michael's mysterious end-time roles is seen to be escorting the dead into the presence of God for judgement. It will be Michael's mission at the end of time to champion the Jewish people as he has always done historically. He would never abandon them and will continue to be their guardian just as he has been the guardian of Moses' body. The body of Moses can be seen as a sacrament representing the entire Jewish people. Michael will be their champion under the Old Covenant.

Finally, because of the sacrifice of the Lamb of God, Jesus Christ, Michael as God's mysterious servant at the end of time, will also be empowered by God to win God's victory. Michael will then enthrone, exalt, and serve Jesus Christ along with the entire heavenly host under the New Covenant. The victory will be God's victory. Who is like God?

NOTES

1. Jerome Biblical Commentary, Raymond E. Brown, S.S., Joseph Fitzmeyer, S.J., Roland Murphy, O. Carm., ed., (Englewood Cliffs, NJ: Prentice Hall Publishing, 1968) Sec 3:12; 77:11–14.

2. Jerome Biblical Commentary, Raymond E. Brown, S.S., Joseph Fitzmeyer, S.J., Roland Murphy, O. Carm., ed., (Englewood Cliffs, NJ: Prentice Hall Publishing, 1968) Sec. 60:11; 64:60; 65:15; 68:14.

3. "Michael?" which discusses the question, "Who is like God?" in Watson E. Mills and Roger A .Bullard, eds., Mercer Dictionary of the Bible (Macon, GA: Mercer University Press, 2nd edition 1990) p. 575.

4. "Angel." Douglas Harper, ed., Online Etymology Dictionary. Found online at http://www.etymonline.com/index.php?search=angel&searchmode=none (Accessed12/17/10).

5. Dn 10:13–22; Dn 12:1; JO 5:13–15; JD 1:9; 2 PTR 2: 10–11; DT 34:6; RV 12:7, New American Bible, St. Joseph Edition, Confraternity of Christian Doctrine, Board of Trustees/National Conference of Catholic Bishops/United States Catholic Conference, Administrative and Editorial Committee/Board (New York, NY: Catholic Book Publishing Co., 1970).

6. Gn 3:24; Num 22:22; 2 Kngs 19:35, New American Bible, St. Joseph Edition, Confraternity of Christian Doctrine, Board of Trustees/National Conference of Catholic Bishops/United States Catholic Conference, Administrative and Editorial Committee/Board (New York, NY: Catholic Book Publishing Co., 1970).

7. "St. Michael, the Archangel." Catholic Encyclopedia, From the New Advent Encyclopedia, found on the New Advent CD-ROM by Kevin Knight (Denver, CO: Advent International, 2009). See also the New Advent website at http://www.newadvent.org/cathen/10275b.htm.

8. Anon., The Book of Enoch, Robert H. Charles, ed., Translated from the Ethiopic text by Professor August Dillman, (Oxford, Eng: Clarendon Press, 1893) Found online at Googlebooks.com. http://books.google.com/books?id=vwA3AAAA MAAJ&printsec=frontcover&dq=the+book+of+enoch&hl=en&ei=10wLTa2tFMP6 8Aa34–SpDg&sa=X&oi=book_result&ct=book-thumbnail&resnum=1&ved=0CDA Q6wEwAA#v=onepage&q&f=false.

9. 1 Qm 11–15, Dead Sea Scrolls, The War of the Sons of Light Against the Sons of Darkness, Florentino Martinez, W. Watson, ed., (Published jointly by Leiden, Neth.: Brill Publishing and Grand Rapids, MI: eeerdmans Publishing, 1996) p. 95. Found online at Googlebooks.com http://books.google.com/books?id=skIJ8NNbzJwC&pg=PA 95&dq=The+war+of+the+sons+of+light+against+the+sons+of+darkness&hl=en&ei= yU4LTc_5FM6s8Ab1r7DJDQ&sa=X&oi=book_result&ct=bookthumbnail&resnum =2&ved=0CCwQ6wEwAQ#v=onepage&q=The%20war%20of%20the%20sons%20 of%20light%20against%20the%20sons%20of%20darkness&f=false.

10. Shepard of Hermas, The Apostolic Fathers, Kirsop Lake, ed. and trans., (New York, NY: G.P. Putnam & Sons, 1917) Found online at Googlebooks.com. See Google books website http://books.google.com/books?id=lqsNAAAAIAAJ&pg=PA1&dq=the +shepherd+of+hermas&hl=en&ei=mFILTfKzN8H8Aa_y435DQ&sa=X&oi=book_res ult&ct=bookthumbnail&resnum=1&ved=0CCkQ6wEwADgK#v=onepage&q&f=false.

11. The Revelation of Moses, Anti-Nicene Fathers, Vol VIII, Rev. Alexander Roberts, Sir James Donaldson, ed., (New York, NY: Cosimo Classics, 2007) p. 565. Found online at Googlebooks.com http://books.google.com/books ?id=518BdgLmXN4C&pg=PA565&dq=the+Revelation+of+Moses+Ante-Nicene &hl=en&ei=eVQLTZzbMMSp8Aac7IWUDg&sa=X&oi=book_result&ct=bookthumbnail&resnum=2&ved=0CDEQ6wEwAQ#v=onepage&q=the%20Revelation%20of%20Moses%20Ante-Nicene&f=false.

12. The Greek Fathers, Adrian Fetesque, ed. (London, Eng.:Catholic Truth Society/Forgotten Books/St Louis, Mo: B. Herder Publ.,1908) Found online at Googlebooks. com. http://books.google.com/books?id=BYdlnpB6_VYC&printsec=frontcover&dq =the+Greek+Fathers&hl=en&ei=T1YLTbvSDcL38Ab6tvG8Dg&sa=X&oi=book_re sult&ct=bookthumbnail&resnum=2&ved=0CCkQ6wEwAQ#v=onepage&q&f=false.

13. Sura 2:98, The Holy Quran, Vol. I, Bashiruddin M. Ahmad, ed. & trans. (Tilford, Surrey, UK: Raqeem press, Islam Int'l., 1988. Found online at Googlebooks. com. See the Googlebooks website http://books.google.com/books?id=RjCfbrXmdb 1C&printsec=frontcover&dq=The+Holy+Quran&hl=en&ei=nVgLTb8OYu8AbPlYz FDQ&sa=X&oi=book_result&ct=bookthumbnail&resnum=4&ved=0CDsQ6wEwA zgK#v=onepage&q&f=false.

14. Who Is The Adventist Jesus?, Elmer Wiebe, ed., (Longwood, Fl: Xulon Publ., 2005) p. 233 Found online at Googlebooks.com. See the Googlebooks website at http://books.google.com/books?id=XmOI3zOrn8MC&pg=PA233&dq=Seventh+ Day+Adventists+Jehovah's+Witnesses+the+archangel+michael&hl=en&ei=wVoL TZnBcT48AbJ_MSZDg&sa=X&oi=book_result&ct=result&resnum=8&ved=0CFI Q6AEwBw#v=onepage&q=Seventh%20Day%20Adventists%20Jehovah's%20Witnesses%20the%20archangel%20michael&f=false.

Section Three

REALITY MEETS MYSTERY
"THIS IS THAT"

Chapter Twenty-Four

Unity of Opposites

MOVING BEYOND DUALITY

In order to understand reality, any relationship between duality and unity must be clarified. Duality, as reality, can only be seen in a unity of opposites or as unity-in-duality. Duality reduces reality to two equally and mutually-opposed principles. Reality is not two realities which have nothing to do with each other, nor is it simply one reality with no regard for its composition or the relationship and distinction of its parts. There must be a unity of any duality in order to visualize a unity of the true nature of reality.

As stated previously, Mythologist Joseph Campbell has said, "Whenever one moves out of the transcendent, one comes into the field of opposites."[1]

A UNITY OF OPPOSITES

A Unity of Opposites can be seen vividly in the Tao, written by Laotse and Chungtse as early as 500 BC. Laotse speaks about how the universe can be pictured as a leveling of all opposites into the One. This can also be seen in Chinese Philosophy with the Yin and the Yang. Yin is seen as the feminine, passive principle in nature. It represents darkness, cold, and wetness. Yin combines with Yang to produce all that comes to be. Yang is the masculine active principle in nature. It represents light, heat, and dryness. Yang combines with Yin to produce all that comes to be. It is impossible to discuss one without reference to its opposite. Yin contains within itself the potential for Yang and Yang for Yin. They are in dynamic equilibrium. If one disappears, the other disappears as well, leaving emptiness.[2]

The principle of The Unity of Opposites has a broad application in the natural world. It implies that "this" is also "that." "That" is also "this." There is nothing which is not "this;" there is nothing which is not "that." "This" emanates from "that;" "that" also derives from "this." There is an interdependence of "this and that." "This is that." "That is this." That the "that" and the "this" cease to be opposites, and are seen in the one unified whole is at the very essence of The Tao. In the Tao, Laotse would write, "Be bent, and you will remain straight. Be vacant, and you will remain full. Be worn, and you will remain new."[3]

One of the unusual occurrences in the development of the principle of the Unity of Opposites was that its development occurred in philosophical thought in different parts of the world at about the same time. For example, while Laotse was writing about it in the Tao, Heraclitus, a philosopher in the Greek world, was writing about it, too.[4] Furthermore the principle appears in the writing of *The Upanishads* in the Hindu world of India.[5] It was also developing in Buddhist thought and these were all occurring simultaneously with no seeming knowledge of one for the other.[6]

In The Unity of Opposites, the principle states that everything in the material world has its opposite; man-woman, I-you, hot-cold, wet-dry, dark-light, life-death, etc. Neither opposite is better than the other, neither stronger than the other, and they are held in dynamic balance in a unifying whole; fully equal.

Similarly, one can also see the continuing development of this principle in Judeo-Christian Theology as well. In both World Religions, God is One and you cannot say one thing about God without saying the opposite. For example, God is transcendent, but God is also imminent. God is big, but God is small too. God is here, but God is everywhere. God is omnipotent, but God also entered the world as a little child. God unifies all opposites in Godself. God is OneGod. However, we believe that God is OneGod in three persons. The Absolute Mystery of the Trinity, is beyond any understanding of duality and still remains shrouded in mystery; not fully revealed to humankind.[7]

THIS IS THAT

by Michael Hickey

I am me
You are you
I couldn't be you
If I wanted to.

You and I are we
To each we are an other
And then there is a they
And they would be another.

Why aren't they a we
Aren't they each the other us?
Doesn't every universal minus-
Find its balance in a plus+?

Is it possible that they
Could conceivably
Be just another you
Or just another me?

I think you might be me
Making me a you
Is one and one then one
Or does that now equal two?

I can't answer who are you
Until I answer who am I
Is that one or two questions?
Do questions end when I die?

I believe that God is One
S/he the Primal Dancer
Don't most questions have
More than just one answer?

Questions and answers
Are a human construct
God still found in silence
Words just obstruct.

NOTES

1. Joseph Campbell, Bill Moyers, The Power of Myth, Betty Flowers, ed., (New York, NY: Anchor Books/Doubleday, 1991).

2. Lin Yutang, The Wisdom of Laotse, (New York, NY: The Modern Library/ Cheng & Tsui Co., 1990) See also The History of Chinese Philosophy, Bo Mou, ed., (New York, NY: Routledge/Taylor & Francis Co., 2009) p. 74. Found online at Googlebooks.com. See the Googlebooks website at http://books.google.com/books?id=wH6jUFojxlUC&pg=PA74&dq=yin+and+yang+chinese+philosophy&hl

=en&ei=Rp8LTcCpAoH58Aai1MX7DQ&sa=X&oi=book_result&ct=result&resnum=4&ved=0CDUQ6AEwAw#v=onepage&q=yin%20and%20yang%20chinese%20philosophy&f=false.

3. Laotse, Tao Te Ching, ch.22, see the Major Religions of the World, Patrick Burke, ed., (Malden, MA: Blackwell Publishing, 2004) p. 176. Found online at Googlebooks.com. http://books.google.com/books?id=Fdh2mcJpFygC&pg=PA176&dq=Be+bent,+and+you+will+remain+straight.+++Be+vacant,+and+you+will+remain+full.++++Be+worn,+and+you+will+remain+new&hl=en&ei=3qELTdiJJsqr8AaF6InyDQ&sa=X&oi=book_result&ct=result&resnum=2&ved=0CCgQ6AEwAQ#v=onepage&q=Be%20bent%2C%20and%20you%20will%20remain%20straight.%20%20%20Be%20vacant%2C%20and%20you%20will%20remain%20full.%20%20%20%20Be%20worn%2C%20and%20you%20will%20remain%20new&f=false.

4. Heraclitus, Heraclitus of Ephesus: Fragments of His Work, G.T.W. Patrick, ed. & trans., (Chicago, IL: Argonaut Publishers, 2006) p.62. Found online at Googlebooks.com http://books.google.com/books?id=T2UrLUcDvfAC&pg=PA62&dq=Heraclitus+unity+of+opposites&hl=en&ei=aqQLTarbEMH98AakuL3rDQ&sa=X&oi=book_result&ct=result&resnum=1&ved=0CCcQ6AEwAA#v=onepage&q=Heraclitus%20unity%20of%20opposites&f=false.

5. The Upanishads, Sri Aurobindo, ed., (Twin Lakes, WI: Lotus Press, 1996) p.19 Found online at Googlebooks.com http://books.google.com/books?id=F0IJMaMTf0cC&pg=PA19&dq= The+Upanishads+Unity+of+opposites&hl=en&ei=OqYLTf_2DoP98AbG8_zDDg&sa=X&oi=book_result&ct=result&resnum=2&ved=0CC0Q6AEwAQ#v=onepage&q&f=false.

6. Buddhism, The Illustrated Guide, Kevin Trainor, ed., (New York, NY: Oxford University Press, 2004) p.197. Found online at Googlebooks.com. See the Googlebooks website at http://books.google.com/books?id=_PrloTKuAjwC&pg=PA197&dq=Buddhism+Unity+of+opposites&hl=en&ei=R6gLTaGMC8L98AaHoLXIDQ&sa=X&oi=book_result&ct=result&resnum=6&ved=0CEQQ6AEwBQ#v=onepage&q&f=false.

7. From the Dogmatic Constitution on the Catholic Faith, Vatican I, 1870. See Richard McBrien, Catholicism, (New York, NY: HarperCollins Publishing, 1994) p. 316. See also "The Trinity." Karl Rahner, Encyclopedia of Theology, The Concise Sacramentum Mundi, Karl Rahner ed., (New York, NY: Seabury/Crossroads Press, 1975) pp. 1755–1771.

Chapter Twenty-Five

Personal and Universal

The word "personal" comes from the Latin *per-sonare* which means "sounding-through." *The Encyclopedia of Theology*, edited by Karl Rahner, defines "person" as "The actual unique reality of a spiritual being. This reality is the reality of a being which belongs to itself and is therefore its own end in itself."[1]

The late Christian spiritual author, Henri Nouwen, has written over 40 best-selling books on the spiritual life. I had the privilege of taking a course in spirituality with him as my instructor at Harvard Divinity School back in the 1980's and got to know him in off-campus settings as well. The course was offered through an affiliation with the Boston Theological Institute. I was attending Weston Jesuit School of Theology/Boston College at the time.

In the course, as well as in several of his inspirational books, one of the things that Henri Nouwen repeated over and over is "What is most personal is most universal."[2]

He believed, as do many other spiritual authors and teachers, that by giving words to our intimate personal experiences, our lives are made more available to others. I maintain that the connection between the personal and universal is not only true in that regard, but that the reality of the connection between the two has implications that ripple. They find their unification beyond the duality of the personal and universal and their intimacy will only be fully known in eternity.

When something is universal it relates to an entire universe of persons. A person is the reality of a being who belongs to itself. To the extent that it controls its own destiny, it is its own end. We only come to a knowledge of our own personhood by contemplating and reflecting on our being in reality with other persons within the context of God as a transcendent reality.

The original definition of "person" dates way back to the Christian theologian, Boethius, who first wrote about the intended meaning back in 550 AD. He made a distinction between person and nature.[3] Thomas Aquinas accepted the definitions and adapted them in the Middle Ages in his *Summa*. "Nature" signifies what a thing is as distinguished from another species of reality; while "person" signifies who it is, i.e. an individual substance of a rational nature.[4]

We cannot understand a personal reality in impersonal terms. This is part of the reason why by our very nature, we as Christians, require a personal relationship with Jesus Christ in The Holy Spirit to grow in the spiritual life. What makes a person a person is not a universal reality in which we all participate, but another person to whom we can relate in our reality. Quoting Teilhard De Chardin,

> To be fully ourselves it is in the opposite direction, in the direction of convergence with the rest, that we must advance—towards the 'other.' The peak of ourselves, the acme of our originality, is not our individuality but our person; and according to the evolutionary structure of the world, we can only find our person by uniting together. There is no mind without synthesis. The same holds good from top to bottom. The true ego grows in inverse proportion to 'egoism.' Like the Omega which attracts it, the element only becomes personal when it universalizes itself.[5]

And . . .

"The human being, if he is honest, will have to recognize that in reality his own 'person' is insufficient for him, and that the most valuable part of his being is precisely what he is still expecting from the unrealized part of the universe."

Also . . .

"But one thing is certain: despite our fears, it is in the direction of 'groupings' that we must advance. The cause of our dislike of collectivity lies in the illusion which makes us stubbornly identify 'personal' with 'individual.'"[6]

We experience our self as a personal reality endowed with consciousness and as part of a universal and transcendent reality who is our personal God. Universal love must have a personal face or else it loses its power in generalities and ambiguity. Its reality is experienced in personality. We most become our "self" when we unite with another "person" in a loving relationship. The mystery of uniting with another person in love, whether that be in marriage, family, or friendship, has universal significance in reality. The self becomes most universal when it personalizes and gets lost in the greater "self." The greater self is not just a personal or universal reality, it is superpersonal and transuniversal.

As human persons, we partake of the living reality of being of God. Man experiences him/herself as a person insofar as s/he becomes conscious of him/herself. The experience of the reality of being a person cannot occur without the movement and acceptance of grace which will begin a questioning process. One asks not only "Who is like God?" One begins also to ask, "What is a human person? Or "Who is my self?" This opens us up to the unlimited horizon created by these questions and thus begins a process of self-transcending or if you would prefer to say the same thing from a different perspective, a process of trans-selfing.

To know who we are as a person in reality, is to gain insight and begin to understand what the ancient Oracle at Delphi might have meant in making the statement, "Know Thyself."[7] Or as the poet Oscar Wilde once quipped, "Only the shallow know themselves."[8] "Knowing thyself," could also give us further insight into the personal and universal implications contained in Jesus words in the gospel, "You shall love the Lord, your God, with all your heart, with all your being, with all your strength, and with all your mind, and your neighbor as yourself." (Lk 10:27)[9]

For, to know oneself as a person is to know other humans as well. The Oracular statement, "Know Thyself," as well as "loving your neighbor as yourself," probably had spiritual and mystical implications, referring to a state of consciousness of the true self. Insight into the words involves a personal and spiritual transformation. Understanding the meaning of the words creates a self-consciousness. This self-consciousness initiates a process of self-transcendence in which there begins to be seen, a phenomenological perception of reality, as well as insight into the mystery of the intimate interconnection between the personal and the universal. What is most personal will be most universal and what is most universal will be most personal.

NOTES

1. "Person." Karl Rahner, Encyclopedia of Theology, The Concise Sacramentum Mundi, Karl Rahner ed., (New York, NY: Seabury/Crossroads Press, 1975) p. 1207.

2. Henri Nouwen, Bread for the Journey: A Daybook of Wisdom and Faith, (New York, NY: HarperCollins Publishing, 1997) p. 23

3. Boethius, Consolation of Philosophy, Hugh Fraser Stewart, Edward Kennard Rand, ed., (New York, NY: G. P. Putnam & Sons, 1918) p. 85. Found online at Googlebooks.com. See Googlebooks http://books.google.com/books?id=rA7gAAA AMAAJ&pg=PA85&dq=boethius+consolation+of+philosophy+definition+person& hl=en&ei=h6UMTbyA8L38Aa2_MiwDg&sa=X&oi=book_result&ct=result&resnu m=1&ved=0CCkQ6AEwAA#v=onepage&q&f=false.

4. Thomas Aquinas, Summa Theologica, Questions 10, 29, 116, From the New Advent Encyclopedia, found on the New Advent CD-ROM by Kevin Knight (Denver, CO: Advent International, 2009). See also the New Advent website at http://www.newadvent.org/utility/search.htm?safe=active&cx=000299817191393086628%3Aifmbhlr-8x0&q=boethius+person+nature&sa=Search&cof=FORID%3A9#799.

5. Pierre Teilhard de Chardin, The Phenomenon of Man, Bernard Wall, ed. (New York, NY: Harper and Row Publishing, 1955) p. 263.

6. Pierre Teilhard de Chardin, Human Energy, The Spirit of the Earth, J. M. Cohen, ed., (New York, NY: Harvest Books, Harcourt Brace Jovanovich, 1962) pp. 31, 64.

7. "Know Thyself" In Greek and Latin Literature, Eliza Gregory Wilkins, ed., (Chicago, IL: University of Chicago Library, & Menasha, WI: Banta Publishing, 1917) p. 45. Found online at Googlebooks.com. See the Googlebooks website at http://books.google.com/books?id=gK1fAAAAMAAJ&pg=PA45&dq=know+thyself+oracle+at+delphi&hl=en&ei=o6sMTd6BD8L8AbVz52yDg&sa=X&oi=book_result&ct=result&resnum=6&ved=0CEMQ6AEwBQ#v=onepage&q&f=false.

8. Oscar Wilde, Phrases and Philosophies for the Use of the Young, 1882, The Annotated Oscar Wilde, Harford Montgomery Hyde, ed., (New York, NY: C. N. Potter/Crown Publishers, 1982) See also Oscar Wilde Quotation online at The Quotation Page, Michael Moncur, ed. At http://www.quotationspage.com/quote/926.html.

9. Lk 10:27, New American Bible, St. Joseph Edition, Confraternity of Christian Doctrine, Board of Trustees/National Conference of Catholic Bishops/United States Catholic Conference, Administrative and Editorial Committee/Board (New York, NY: Catholic Book Publishing Co., 1970).

Chapter Twenty-Six

Matter and Spirit

Everything that moves in the world has some form of dynamic energy. *Einstein's Theory of Relativety (E=MC2)* tells us that all matter is comprised of some form of energy and that all matter in the universe is either slowly or quickly transforming into energy.[1]

In the broadest sense, matter can be seen as just plain stuff that occupies space. When viewing the human being as matter, however, it is then that matter becomes something more. The word, "matter," in its etymology comes from the Latin, *materia,* which is "the something from which something is made." In fact, the root of the word is *mater*, in the Latin, which means "mother."[2] The human, as a material being, is a spacial and temporal being, situated in history and reality. The act of being is rooted in matter as its reality. So, we are humans, whose acts of being are realized essence or spirit in matter.

In the human sense, matter can be seen as the self-revealing, outward expression of the existence of the human spirit in space and time. Existence and essence are not the same. Neither is matter and spirit two natures united, but rather their union forms one single nature. We have a "graced nature."[3] A human being realizes their humanity in the union of spirit and matter. We are, at one and the same time, a real mystery and a mysterious reality.

In terms of the union of spirit and matter as one human reality; God, as a transcendent reality, is not the supreme union of all the reality that is produced by this union. Rather, God is the ultimate ground of all reality including this union. In other words, God, as Wholly Other, is not simply the sum of all the worldly spirit and matter parts.

The word "spirit" came into our language from the Latin, *spiritus,* which means "breath." It was originally translated in the scriptures from *ruah, H.; pneuma, Gk*; both of which meant "breath." Breath is life.[4] With each breath, we as humans participate in the living energy of the universe. Breathing is mostly an unconscious process, though we begin breathing at birth and don't stop until the day we die. We breathe without actually doing it and most of the time without ever being conscious of doing it. We are not only human beings, we are "human breathings."

So, spirit can be seen as the life principle and dynamic energy within living things. It is in the orientation of ourselves as human beings, to the Absolute Being, who is Spirit, that self-transcending takes place. This makes us really human, while at the same time it is mysteriously transforming our being. Through the movement of grace and orientation to God in self-transcendence, both spirit and matter have the potential to be transformed.

As human beings, we are creatures whose existence needs to make sense to us. But, because we are human beings, we do not simply exist. We also have an essence which is our very nature as opposed to our existence. Essence is our "is-ness" or state of being; it is what makes us human and provides the shape, form, or purpose to us as matter. Essence and matter need each other. It is essence which makes matter real. Essence "realizes" matter and essence "spiritualizes" matter. So that we are, at one and the same time, both real embodied spirits and mysterious spiritized bodies.

To quote Karl Rahner,

> Man is one substance, but in such a way that his unity is ontologically prior to, and comprises, a real and genuine, irreducible plurality of essential composition. Man is one by origin, nature and last end. Consequently no statement can be made about anything in him, about one component in the plurality of his essential constitution. This can be quite without significance for the rest of him, nor could any statement be adequate even in a limited way, unless its actual precise meaning were drawn from its relation to the one human being in his unity.[5]

The embodiment of the spiritual in the material and the communication of the spiritual through the material could be called a "sacramental mystery" in that it is a visible sign of an invisible reality. As Matter and Spirit, Jesus was and is the great Sacrament of God. We, as Christians, who are matter and spirit, are a Sacrament of Christ because the Holy Spirit is in us.

But, in the end, "spirit" and "matter" are merely words, as are "reality" and "mystery." We, as human beings, through grace, give life and meaning to the words. The words, even though real, will die a static death in time, like us. Matter and spirit are in union within the human person; however, we as humans view things in duality in a field of opposites.

Quoting Teilhard de Chardin:

> You can well imagine, accordingly, how strong was my inner feeling of release and expansion when I took my first still hesitant steps into an 'evolutive' uni-

verse, and saw that the dualism in which I had hitherto been enclosed was disappearing like the mist before the rising sun. Matter and spirit: these were no longer two things, but two states, or two aspects of one and the same cosmic stuff.[6]

If I were to consider one word in our language which could analogously describe the union of spirit and matter in its unified reality, eliminating the perceived duality and capable of transformation, it would be the word "seed." We are seeds. All that is our reality will eventually be dying into the mystery. However, even in turning to dust, we will still be beloved dust. We will contain both the substance and the dynamic energy of the Creator. The God who is our source can only be our end, Father, Son, and Holy Spirit. As is written in the Scripture, "We know not what we shall be, but we know that when He shall appear, we will be like Him, for we shall see Him as He is *(1Jn 3:2–3)*."[7]

NOTES

1. Albert Einstein, Relativety: The Special and General Theory, Robert Lawson, ed. and trans., (New York, NY: Henry Holt & co, 1920) Found online at Googlebooks.com. http://books.google.com/books?id=3H46AAAAMAAJ&printsec=frontcover&dq=albert+einstein+theory+of+relativity&hl=en&ei=BgYNTZ-hMYT68AbM-ozxDQ&sa=X&oi=book_result&ct=book-thumbnail&resnum=1&ved=0CDcQ6wEwAA#v=onepage&q&f=false.

2. "Matter." Douglas Harper, ed., Online Etymology Dictionary. Found online at http://www.etymonline.com/index.php?search=matter&searchmode=none.

3. "Grace" and "Nature," Catholic Encyclopedia, From the New Advent Encyclopedia, found on the New Advent CD-ROM by Kevin Knight (Denver, CO: Advent International, 2009). See also the New Advent website at http://www.newadvent.org/cathen/06701a.htm and http://www.newadvent.org/cathen/10715a.htm.

4. "Spirit." Douglas Harper, ed., Online Etymology Dictionary. Found online at http://www.etymonline.com/index.php?search=spirit&searchmode=none.

5. Karl Rahner, Hominization:The Evolutionary Origin of Man as a Theological Problem, W. T. O'Hara, ed. and trans., (New York, NY: Herder & Herder, 1965) Sec. 1.

6. Pierre Teilhard de Chardin, The Heart of Matter, Helen and Kurt Woolf, Rene Hague, ed. and trans., (Boston, MA: Houghton Mifflin Harcourt, 2002) p. 26.

7. 1Jn 3:2–3, New American Bible, St. Joseph Edition, Confraternity of Christian Doctrine, Board of Trustees/National Conference of Catholic Bishops/United States Catholic Conference, Administrative and Editorial Committee/Board (New York, NY: Catholic Book Publishing Co., 1970).

Chapter Twenty-Seven

Nature and Grace

The word "nature," is derived from the Latin word "natura," meaning "to be born."[1] Nature, for the most part, is not a Biblical concept but has evolved from theological reflection on the New Testament, primarily in the letters of Paul and John.[2] The theological concept of nature stems from the revealed truth of the divinization of man by the grace of Christ found first in the New Testament, then being carried through the writings of the early fathers and early theologians such as Augustine and Boethius. Subsequently, it would find its foundation in the Middle Ages, especially in the *Summa Theologica* of Thomas Aquinas.[3]

To see nature as separate from grace is also to have a dualistic view of the universe. To see them as gracednature is to see them as parts of the same whole. Grace supposes nature while at one and the same time, nature supposes grace. Grace can be viewed as the presence and self-communication of God. When it is spoken of as "sanctifying grace," it becomes the presence and self-communication of God within the human person. Nature can be viewed as the human condition apart from grace, but with the radical capacity to receive grace. But, "pure nature" without the radical capacity to receive grace does not exist. It is simply a logical construct one can only make in the mind. One cannot make a distinction between nature and grace; the two are inseparable because all reality is radically graced and the entire real, historical order is already permeated with grace. God is present to all that is. To view grace any other way would be to see it as an add-on to nature, which it is not.[4]

It is true, of course, that in the New Testament, the grace of God appears in Christ for our salvation (Titus 2:11), and by grace, Jesus suffered and died for all (Heb 2:9).[5] Grace, in Christ, certainly has a salvific dimension. Occasionally, however, some Christians will so over-emphasize the superiority of grace over nature that what gets seemingly lost is the freedom inherent in the nature of the human person to cooperate with Christ in God's entire plan of salvation. The history of the world is at one-and-the-same time the history of salvation.

The meaning and intention of grace is wider in scope and can be described, not only in its salvific dimension, but more as "that which is given." The Greek word for grace in the New Testament is "charis" which means not only "grace," but "gift."[6] A "gift" is "that which is given (James 4:6)."[7] And God is not just conferring created gifts as a token of his love; it is God's self-communication. God is communicating Godself so that we can not only share in the grace, but also in the very nature of God. The evidence and highest realization of this mystery was, and is, the GracedNature of Jesus Christ; God in Christ.

Sin, because it also involves the freedom inherent in our human nature, works against grace, but it can never, under any circumstances, destroy grace within our nature. As has been stated earlier, grace is not separate or an add-on to our nature. Because of our gracednature, the sinner remains still yet always radically open to the possibilities of conversion, repentance, and forgiveness of sin. Grace supposes, even in the sinner, nature and the natural capacity to receive the grace. But alas, because of free-will in the nature of the human person, the grace can either be accepted or rejected.[8]

NOTES

1. "Nature." Douglas Harper, ed., Online Etymology Dictionary. Found online at http://www.etymonline.com/index.php?search=nature&searchmode=none.

2. "Nature." Jerome Biblical Commentary, Raymond E. Brown, S.S., Joseph Fitzmeyer, S.J., Roland Murphy, O. Carm., ed., (Englewood Cliffs, NJ: Prentice Hall Publishing, 1968) Sec. 77:47–102.

3. "Nature" and "Grace," Catholic Encyclopedia, From the New Advent Encyclopedia, found on the New Advent CD-ROM by Kevin Knight (Denver, CO: Advent International, 2009). See also the New Advent website at http://www.newadvent.org/fathers/1503.htm And for Thomas Aquinas, Summa, see Questions 109 and 113, New Advent Website at http://www.newadvent.org/summa/2109.htm and http://www.newadvent.org/summa/2113.htm.

4. "Nature and Grace" in Richard P. McBrien, ed., Catholicism: Study Edition (Minneapolis, MN: Winston Press, 1981 and New York, NY: HarperCollins Publishers, 1994) pp. 129, 134, 146, 151–167, 225–226, 298, 309, 324–325, 463, 753, 910–911, 1068, 1120–1121, 1128–1133, 1174, 1183.

5. Titus 2:11; Heb 2:9, New American Bible, St. Joseph Edition, Confraternity of Christian Doctrine, Board of Trustees/National Conference of Catholic Bishops/United States Catholic Conference, Administrative and Editorial Committee/Board (New York, NY: Catholic Book Publishing Co., 1970).

6. "Charism." Douglas Harper, ed., Online Etymology Dictionary. Found online at http://www.etymonline.com/index.php?search=charism&searchmode=none.

7. James 4:6, New American Bible, St. Joseph Edition, Confraternity of Christian Doctrine, Board of Trustees/National Conference of Catholic Bishops/United States Catholic Conference, Administrative and Editorial Committee/Board (New York, NY: Catholic Book Publishing Co., 1970).

8. "Grace" and "Sin." Encyclopedia of Theology, The Concise Sacramentum Mundi, Karl Rahner ed., (New York, NY: Seabury/Crossroads Press, 1975) pp. 584–601; 1579–1590.

Chapter Twenty-Eight

Natural and Supernatural

Nature has reference to the production of things, and hence generally includes in its connotation the ideas of energy and activity. In philosophy, nature and essence are closely related terms. Aristotle has said, "Nature properly speaking is the essence (or substance) of things which have in themselves as such a principle of activity."[1]

Only in God is essence and existence the same because "God IS good (Ps 25:8, 34:8; Mk 10:18)" and "God IS love (1 Jn 4:8)."[2] So, if the essence of our being is not perfection, as is the case with God, the essence of our being must of necessity be change. This would make us both existential human beings and essential human becomings as well. Because reality is not a static concept, but is dynamic and evolutionary, we are essentially "realizing" our essence in reality. On the other hand, because our true essence as a human person is not yet fully "realized," but will be only in the future, it is at one and the same time, a mystery to us.

In his book *A Rumor of Angels*, sociologist Peter L. Berger writes about modern society and the rediscovery of the supernatural. In his 3rd chapter, titled *Theological Possibilities Starting With Man,* he argues for the existence of a realm of the supernatural based on certain "signals of transcendence" that exist within the natural realm and human nature. Perhaps his most interesting argument, I found to be the *Argument From Humor.*

Humor, as a phenomenon, has existed within the nature of man since the beginning of time. Humor is based on discrepancy, incongruity, irony, and absurdity. Something is considered humorous when it belongs to two altogether independent series of events and is capable of being interpreted with two entirely different meanings at the same time. For example, discrepancy is what makes a joke humorous because the punch line reveals an entirely different meaning.

By laughing, we transcend the present or the "what is" of reality. Humor within the nature of man can possibly indicate another reality, for it points to the ultimate discrepancies being between man and God, the natural and supernatural. To quote Berger,

> The comic reflects the imprisonment of the human spirit in the world. This is why, as has been pointed out over and over since classical antiquity, comedy and tragedy are at root closely related. . . . Humor implies that the imprisonment is not final but will be overcome.[3]

God exists as a transcendent reality and the free cause of nature. The supernatural is that which exceeds the power and capacity of our human nature apart from grace. The supernatural is also the realm of the spirit, with as little materiality as possible. It affects external and internal actions in reality that are beyond the power and capacity of our limited humanity. It is also beyond our full understanding and comprehension. Therefore, the supernatural in any ultimate understanding of the term can only be more mystery than reality for us. For us, in our humanity, there can neither exist a purely natural state nor a state of pure reality. So, "grace will follow nature" and "nature will suppose grace" as Aquinas would write in his *Summa Theologica*.[4]

In our earthly reality, nature cannot exist as pure nature apart from grace. So, it is grace which orients the natural toward the supernatural. This can create an experience for us in our reality of God's self-communication and our self-transcendence. This occurs as natural encounters supernatural and reality encounters mystery. What is implicit in this is that because of the life, death, and resurrection of Jesus Christ and the grace of Christ in us, our spirit has then been oriented to the Holy Spirit as the ground of our entire reality.

Our reality is mysteriously becoming one in Christ and will find its ending in Christ. To use Karl Rahner's language, we are becoming what he calls a "supernatural existential."[5] Our radical capacity for God is permanently modifying our human nature and reality in the very depths of our being. Our spirit is being transformed from within and oriented to the supernatural through God's gift of a graced nature. This does not necessarily make us conscious of the grace as grace. As Rahner would argue, "Experiencing grace is different than experiencing grace as grace."[6]

It still remains as mystery because God is "Holy Mystery" and our experience of the supernatural is always the experience of a transcendent reality. We can only be aware of the supernatural to the extent that the Spirit of God, the Holy Spirit in us, tells us. This can occur not only through reading what is said about the supernatural in the scriptures, but also through spiritual experiences. This tells us that more may be going on within our human nature than we may realize at any point in time. Our faith must remain in the unseen, because our hope is as yet unrealized, that love will be all there is for us in the end. Through the experience of loving and being loved we experience both a natural reality and a profound supernatural mystery.

SUPERNATURAL EXISTENTIAL

by Michael Hickey

Supernatural Existential,
Nature, supposing grace,
Spirit's full potential,
Offered to the human race.
Becoming into being,
Self-transcending anthropoid,
Material spirit, spiritual matter,
Orienting unto God.
Man's freedom to accept,
Transformation from within;
Man's freedom to reject,
Overcoming of all sin.
Radical love and knowledge,
Brought into human history;
The offer of himself within;
God in his Holy Mystery
Encounter with the thou
and with the total other,
Communion in the now,
Wholly Father, Holy Mother.

NOTES

1. Aristotle, Metaphysics, 1015a, On Aristotle's Metaphysics: an Annotated Translation, Averroes, Rudiger Amzen, ed. (New York, NY: Walter de Gruyter Publishing, 2010).
2. Ps 25:8; 34:8; Mk 10:18; 1 Jn 4:8, New American Bible, St. Joseph Edition, Confraternity of Christian Doctrine, Board of Trustees/National Conference of Catholic Bishops/United States Catholic Conference, Administrative and Editorial Committee/Board (New York, NY: Catholic Book Publishing Co., 1970).
3. Peter Berger, Rumor of Angels: Modern Society and the Rediscovery of the Supernatural, (New York, NY: Doubleday & Co./Anchor Books, 1970) ch. 3/Theological Possibilities Starting With Man.
4. Thomas Aquinas, Summa Theologica, Questions 2 and 109, From the New Advent Encyclopedia, found on the New Advent CD-ROM by Kevin Knight (Denver,

CO: Advent International, 2009). See also the New Advent website at http://www.newadvent.org/summa/1002.htm and http://www.newadvent.org/summa/2109.htm.

5. Karl Rahner, "Supernatural Existential" in Richard P. McBrien, ed., Catholicism: Study Edition (Minneapolis, MN: Winston Press, 1981 and New York, NY: HarperCollins Publishers, 1994) pp. 160–161, 183, 191–195, 222–225, 233, 267, 319, 1104.

6. Karl Rahner, Theological Investigations, Volume 1, and "Grace" Encyclopedia of Theology, The Concise Sacramentum Mundi, Karl Rahner ed., (New York, NY: Seabury/Crossroads Press, 1975) pp. 584–601. See also Karl Rahner, Nature and Grace: Dilemmas in the Modern Church, (Lanham MD: Sheed & Ward/Rowman & Littlefield Publishing, 1964).

Chapter Twenty-Nine

Heaven and Earth

"Thy will be done on earth as it is in heaven."(Mt 6:10)[1]

It would be an over-simplification to state that heaven is the abode of God; where God lives as Holy Mystery, and the earth is where we live out our reality as human persons. First, because God is everywhere and his presence permeates everything. Second, because our reality on earth is to be living somewhere between the Kingdom of Heaven time, which is already mysteriously "in our midst," and the eternal Kingdom of Heaven which is not yet fully realized.

"Earth, globe, and world," are the most common terms we use to describe the planet on which we dwell. The term, "globe" when used often emphasizes the roundness of the earth. "World," when used, emphasizes the inhabitants of the earth, their activities, interests, and concerns. "Globe and world," are most often inclusive terms. "Earth" is both inclusive and exclusive. We use the term "earth," in particular, to describe our 3rd planet from the sun and to distinguish earth from other planets in our galaxy. However, we also use the term "earth," when we want to contrast our existence with that of "heaven." Earth and heaven are perceived as a duality.[2]

In its etymology, the word "earth," comes from the Old English, "eorðe" which means "ground, soil, or dry land." "Heaven" comes through many Gothic and Old English words which generally translate it to mean, "the roof of the world." It is also a condition of perfect happiness or bliss and the completion of all we are as human persons in likeness to Christ and so to God.[3]

In the incarnation of Jesus Christ, the love of God unites heaven and earth, and they begin to lose all duality. Through his death and resurrection, Jesus has opened heaven for us. We are becoming the blessed community incorporated into Christ in heaven. By his dying and rising, Jesus Christ has effected a cosmic reconciliation of both heaven and earth (COL 1:20–21) and through Christ, we as Christians, in union with him, sit down with Christ in the heavenly realm (EPH 2:5–6).[4]

It was common for the ancient Hebrew to substitute the word "heaven" for the word "God." As was discussed earlier, Jews were very cautious in avoiding the use of the divine name. In the New Testament, this is found most frequently in Matthew's gospel as he refers to "the Kingdom of Heaven" and not "the Kingdom of God" as the gospel writer Mark had done before him. The Kingdom of Heaven, as Matthew refers to it, has already been initiated. It is in our midst, come near, or "at hand," (MT 4:17; 13:45; 16:19). With the coming of Jesus Christ, it was a profound mystery that had already entered reality.

In Pauline thought, there were actually three heavens (2 COR 12). The first heaven, was the earth and its atmosphere (GEN 1:9–10; DT 4:17). The second heaven consisted of the region of the stars (GEN 1: 14–17). And the third heaven was equated with Paradise and was the place where God was seen to dwell (2 COR 12:2).

How heaven functions, where it is, what is the beatific vision, what kind of glorified body will we have, how heaven is fully distinguished from earth, and questions of this nature all remain a mystery. On the other hand, to view heaven as a totally distinct realm, separated from earth and the reality of our earthly existence, is to create another duality. Earth and heaven are one inseparable reality. There is one Kingdom and it is God's. This Kingdom exists now and is coming to be in the history of the world. The Kingdom of Heaven is upon us, being manifested in the movement of The Holy Spirit and in the mystery and reality of our loving relationships with one another here on earth.

"Heaven and earth will pass away, but my words will not pass away (MK 13:31)."[5]

NOTES

1. Mt 6:10, New American Bible, St. Joseph Edition, Confraternity of Christian Doctrine, Board of Trustees/National Conference of Catholic Bishops/United States Catholic Conference, Administrative and Editorial Committee/Board (New York, NY: Catholic Book Publishing Co., 1970).

2. "Earth; Globe; World; Heaven." Webster's Ninth New Collegiate Dictionary, Hubert Kelsey, ed., (Springfield, MA: Merriam-Webster Inc., Publishers, 1990) pp. 392, 521, 1360, 560.

3. "Earth and Heaven." Douglas Harper, ed., Online Etymology Dictionary. Found online at http://www.etymonline.com/index.php?search=earth&searchmode=none and http://www.etymonline.com/index.php?search=heaven&searchmode=none.

4. COL 1:20–21; EPH 2:5–6, New American Bible, St. Joseph Edition, Confraternity of Christian Doctrine, Board of Trustees/National Conference of Catholic Bishops/United States Catholic Conference, Administrative and Editorial Committee/Board (New York, NY: Catholic Book Publishing Co., 1970).

5. "Heaven, God, Kingdom of Heaven, Kingdom of God." MT 4:17; 13:45; 16:19; 2 COR 12; GEN 1:9–10; DT 4:17; GEN 1: 14–17; 2 COR 12:2; MK 13:31, New American Bible, St. Joseph Edition, Confraternity of Christian Doctrine, Board of Trustees/National Conference of Catholic Bishops/United States Catholic Conference, Administrative and Editorial Committee/Board (New York, NY: Catholic Book Publishing Co., 1970). See also Jerome Biblical Commentary, Raymond E. Brown, S.S., Joseph Fitzmeyer, S.J., Roland Murphy, O. Carm., ed., (Englewood Cliffs, NJ: Prentice Hall Publishing, 1968) Sec. 52:42, pp. 288–289.

Chapter Thirty

Time and Eternity

It is heaven which is considered as "eternal life." The Christian faith confesses that the earth had a beginning in time and that there will come an end to time and all world history as we know it on earth. As discussed previously, theologians have referred to this as "The Omega Point."[1] Scripture also uses the words, "the fullness of time," to speak about this mystery. The Apostle Paul writes, "In all wisdom and insight, God has made known to us the mystery of his will in accord with his favor that he set forth in him as a plan for the fullness of times, to sum up all things in Christ in heaven and on earth (EPH 1:9–10)."[2]

Time is the system of those sequential relations that any event has to any other as past, present, or future. It is a definitive measure as ascertained by a clock or a calendar, for example. It also distinguishes duration which belongs to the present life as distinct from the life to come or from eternity. In time, the present is never completely detached from the past or the future. The present reflects the past and is open to the future. Yesterday and tomorrow would lose all meaning in "reality" if there were no today. But eternity is not just the running on from time.

Eternity is a measurement of that which is perfectly whole and lasts forever without beginning or end. It is symbolized by the circle and can be visualized as a perfect, living circle. It is always existing, perpetual, ceaseless, endless, and exists outside of and beyond all measurements of time. It is not subject to change or alteration. Eternity is imperishable, indestructible, undying, and deathless.

Aristotle, in discussing what he referred to as an "Eternal Prime Mover," maintained that: "The principles of eternal things must be always most true, for they are not merely sometimes true, nor is there any cause of their being, but they themselves are the cause of the being of other things, so that each thing is in respect of being, so it is in respect of truth." And also, "God is a living being, eternal, most good, so that life and duration, continuous and eternal, belong to God; for this is God."[3]

The original Christian definition of "eternity" can be traced to the Christian lay theologian Boethius in 480 AD: "It is perfect life, without succession, beginning, or end."[4]

Both Augustine and Aquinas after him, have said, "God is the author of eternity."[5]

What is eternally enduring and permanent can be accomplished by God in a single moment in time. God knows the past and the future; however, God is eternally present. The ancient Greeks had two words for time, "*chronos*" and "*kairos*." The former referred to chronological or sequential time. The latter referred to undetermined, unsequential time, without beginning or end, in which something special happened. Chronos was quantitative and kairos was qualitative. Kairos could be considered "Kingdom time."[6]

In the New Testament, kairos refers to "the appointed time in the purpose of God (MK 1:15)." It concerns time as it intersects with eternity. The coming of Jesus Christ in history is a prime example. The ancient Hebrew also contrasted "et," which is fixed time and "olan," which originally implied a very long period of time that perdured through centuries or ages (GEN 17:9) and much later took on the additional meaning of something outside of time, such as timelessness or eternity (1 John 5:11–12).

There is a theological measurement of time, which regards time in the context of God's offer of salvation and man's freedom of decision. Time, in this regard, is considered to be a measurement of salvation history. Salvation history is the history of the world in which God progressively brings man toward the kingdom of heaven or eternal life. It begins with creation and ends with the second coming of Christ. The climactic moment of all history will always be the event of Jesus Christ. Because of the life, death, and resurrection of Jesus, all of history is somehow bound for glory and not simply the finality of time.

As the scriptures tell us, "God is love, and whoever remains in love remains in God and God in him (1 Jn 4:16)" and "So faith, hope, love remain, these three; but the greatest of these is love (1 Cor 13:13)."

Love is eternal and is all there is in the end. Whenever any life is lived in faith, hope, and love, and manifests the fruit of the Spirit, (Gal. 5:22), eternity is occuring in time. Something more is occuring other than what can be seen and experienced in the hereness and nowness of time.[7]

NOTES

1. Pierre Teilhard de Chardin, The Phenomenon of Man, Bernard Wall, ed. (New York, NY: Harper and Row Publishing, 1959) pp. 57, 257–264, 268–272, 288, 291–298, 307–309.

2. EPH 1:9–10, New American Bible, St. Joseph Edition, Confraternity of Christian Doctrine, Board of Trustees/National Conference of Catholic Bishops/United States Catholic Conference, Administrative and Editorial Committee/Board (New York, NY: Catholic Book Publishing Co., 1970).

3. Aristotle, Metaphysics, BK II, sec 1; BK XII, sec. 7, Aristote's Metaphysics, Hugh Lawson Tancred, ed. & trans., (New York, NY: Penguin Books/Putnam, 1998).

4. "Eternity." Boethius, Consolation of Philosophy, BK V, sec. 6, Hugh Fraser Stewart, Edward Kennard Rand, ed., (New York, NY: G. P. Putnam & Sons, 1918) See also Brian Leftow, ed., Time & Eternity, (Ithaca, NY: Cornell University Press, 1991) pp. 113–118. Found online at http://books.google.com/books?id=99jYAAAA MAAJ&q=%E2%80%9Ceternity%E2%80%9D+Boethius+consolation+of+philoso phy.&dq=%E2%80%9Ceternity%E2%80%9D+Boethius+consolation+of+philosop hy.&hl=en&ei=yUsPTcjTG4GB8ga62ODvDQ&sa=X&oi=book_result&ct=result& resnum=2&ved=0CCkQ6AEwAQ.

5. Augustine, Confessions, Book XI, Thomas Aquinas, Summa Theologica, Question 10, Articles 1–6, From the New Advent Encyclopedia, found on the New Advent CD-ROM by Kevin Knight (Denver, CO: Advent International, 2009). See also the New Advent website at http://www.newadvent.org/summa/1010.htm#article1.

6. Jerome Biblical Commentary, Raymond E. Brown, S.S., Joseph Fitzmeyer, S.J., Roland Murphy, O. Carm., ed., (Englewood Cliffs, NJ: Prentice Hall Publishing, 1968) Sec.48:26–53:125.

7. MK 1:15; GEN 17:9; 1 John 5:11–12; 1 Cor 13:13; 1 Jn 4:16; Gal 5:22, New American Bible, St. Joseph Edition, Confraternity of Christian Doctrine, Board of Trustees/National Conference of Catholic Bishops/United States Catholic Conference, Administrative and Editorial Committee/Board (New York, NY: Catholic Book Publishing Co., 1970).

Chapter Thirty-One

Knowing and Unknowing

The only God worth knowing is the God who cannot be known. The only God worth speaking about is the God that cannot be put into words. Although this God cannot be spoken about, he can be spoken to and listened to.

God is all-knowing. Only God knows fully and with complete certainty, because God is the creator of everyone and everything. God is also the source of the illumination of the mind which leads to true knowledge and the discovery of eternal truths. We can infer and intuit from what is known in the visible and material world of reality, what is unknown in the invisible and spiritual world of mystery. As Paul would write, "At present we see indistinctly, as in a mirror, but then face to face. At present I know partially; then I shall know fully, as I am fully known (1 Cor 13: 12)."

Something or someone is known when it is perceived, comprehended, and understood as fact or truth. Knowing involves judgement, explicit or implicit, and includes the process of distinguishing, therefore there must be clear and unambiguous certainty of the mind and memory or an awareness of a subject or object by sight or personal experience.

Knowledge, however, is not synonymous with consciousness. As Karl Rahner, Teilhard de Chardin, and other noted theologians have indicated, we can know something yet not be fully conscious of it. Both Hegel and Karl Rahner have also said, "All questions about knowledge are themselves knowledge."[1]

The modern understanding of "knowing," is often based on a series of propositions and the relationship of certain propositions to elements of reality comprehended and understood. Propositions, however, can be correct in formal logic, but not necessarily in accord with reality. Hence they would not necessarily be knowledge. Truth is a prerequisite for knowledge. Both truth and knowledge must be in accord with reality.

In his *Summa Theologica,* Thomas Aquinas would write, "When a man by his natural reason, assents by his intellect to some truth, he is perfected in two ways in respect to that truth: first, because he grasps it; secondly because he forms a sure judgement on it."
And,

> Accordingly, since the word knowledge implies certitude of judgement, if this certitude of the judgement is derived from the highest cause, the knowledge has a special name, which is wisdom: for a wise man in any branch of knowledge is one who knows the highest cause of that kind of knowledge and is able to judge of all matters by that cause: and a wise man 'absolutely.' is one who knows the cause which is absolutely highest which is God. Hence the knowledge of divine things is called 'wisdom, while the knowledge of human things is called 'knowledge.'

Aquinas would also maintain, "Faith presupposes natural knowledge, even as grace presupposes nature."[2]

Conceptual knowledge does not exist on its own. It is interwoven into a complex of basic acts and our experience of the truth. In judging, we know conceptually when we compare, discriminate, identify, and connect. Certain factors, such as experience, observation, and thought also assist in the process.

To the ancient Hebrew mind, true knowledge came from the experience of a person and not conceptual knowledge. In the New Testament early Christian church, however, knowledge was understood by the Greek word, "epignosis," which to the Greek world originally had implied an understanding of the universe and its workings. When the Apostle Paul uses the word in his letters, he is conveying an intended meaning of a certain "Christian epignosis." To Paul, this was a knowledge of God's will and divine mind, manifested in saving mankind in Christ.[3] It was not conceptual knowledge, but a personal knowledge of God himself (COL 1:9–10, 2:2) through being conformed to the image and likeness of Jesus Christ (COL 3:10). Paul is conveying a Christian understanding of personal knowledge more in line with the ancient Hebrew mind as opposed to the prevailing Greek concept of knowledge prevalent in the ancient Hellenistic world.[4]

When something or someone is unknown, it is not within the range of our knowledge, perception or understanding. It or they are strange, unfamiliar, undiscovered, unidentified, or uncertain. Whereas the known is often represented by the first few letters of the alphabet (knowing the ABC's of something), the unknown is often represented by the last few letters of the alphabet (X factor, object Y, zone Z).

Knowledge is not always morally neutral. As one of the seven "Gifts of the Holy Spirit," (1 Cor 12:7–10), knowledge in its fullness, belongs to Christ. It assists in completing and perfecting our virtue and character and shapes our ultimate destiny. Therefore, knowledge can only be good and beneficial when it is disposed to do good and is oriented to God. It is the virtue of prudence which gives us the ability to discern, deliberate, distinguish and decide what knowledge is disposed to good and what knowledge is disposed to what is not good. Nuclear power, for example, can either heat homes or build bombs. And since the mythical Garden of Eden, in the Book of Genesis (GEN 3:1–24), we have been told that there are some things that are best left "unknown." An example here would be knowing another person in an adulterous affair, while ruining a long-standing, loving marriage or knowing what it is like to take hard drugs.[5]

All knowledge, including our concept of knowledge, is based on our experience, and first and last on our experience of truth as it relates to reality of being and our own individual essence.

Truth is concrete in moral acts and personal love. Therefore it is essential that love should always, and in every act, have primacy to knowledge. We must, in truth, be made true lovers before we can, in reality, be made real knowers. We are told in 1 Cor 8:1: "Knowledge inflates with pride, but love builds up."[6] Furthermore, because love does have primacy to knowledge, one must "love thyself," before one can "know thyself."

Because God resides more in profound mystery than in our reality, our knowledge of God can only be realized more fully in our unknowing of God than in our knowing of God. "The Cloud of Unknowing," an anonymous mystical classic written in the latter half of the fourteenth century, is a spiritual guide on contemplative prayer which counsels the reader not to seek God through knowledge, but through simple love. Echoing the scripture verse above, the writer says, "On account of pride, knowledge may often deceive you, but this gentle loving affection will not deceive you. Knowledge tends to breed conceit, but love builds." The writer goes on to quote St. Denis in chapter 70 by saying, "The most goodly knowing of God, is that which is known by unknowing."[7]

In a more modern example, the writer and poet, T. S. Eliot, a generation ago, penned these words in his *Choruses From the Rock:* "Where is the life we have lost in living? Where is the wisdom we have lost in knowledge? Where is the knowledge we have lost in information?" He was indeed prophetic, as today we live in what is called, "The Information Age."[8]

NOTES

1. Karl Rahner, Encyclopedia of Theology, The Concise Sacramentum Mundi, Karl Rahner ed., (New York, NY: Seabury/Crossroads Press, 1975) p. 801.

2. Thomas Aquinas, Summa Theologica, Question 9, Ans. 1 and 2, and Question 2, Article 2, From the New Advent Encyclopedia, found on the New Advent CD-ROM by Kevin Knight (Denver, CO: Advent International, 2009). See also the New Advent website at http://www.newadvent.org/summa/1002.htm and http://www.newadvent.org/summa/3009.htm.

3. Jerome Biblical Commentary, Raymond E. Brown, S.S., Joseph Fitzmeyer, S.J., Roland Murphy, O. Carm., ed., (Englewood Cliffs, NJ: Prentice Hall Publishing, 1968) Sec. 55:11, p.336.

4. 1 Cor 13: 12; COL 1:9–10; 2:2; 3:10, New American Bible, St. Joseph Edition, Confraternity of Christian Doctrine, Board of Trustees/National Conference of Catholic Bishops/United States Catholic Conference, Administrative and Editorial Committee/Board (New York, NY: Catholic Book Publishing Co., 1970).

5. 1 Cor 12:7–10; GEN 3:1–24, New American Bible, St. Joseph Edition, Confraternity of Christian Doctrine, Board of Trustees/National Conference of Catholic Bishops/United States Catholic Conference, Administrative and Editorial Committee/Board (New York, NY: Catholic Book Publishing Co., 1970). See also Catechism of the Catholic Church, Geoffrey Chapman, ed., (London, UK: Burns & Oates/Continuum Publishing Group, 1999) #1831.

6. "Love Has Primacy to Knowledge." Karl Rahner, Encyclopedia of Theology, The Concise Sacramentum Mundi, Karl Rahner ed., (New York, NY: Seabury/Crossroads Press, 1975) p. 58. See also 1 Cor 8:1, New American Bible, St. Joseph Edition, Confraternity of Christian Doctrine, Board of Trustees/National Conference of Catholic Bishops/United States Catholic Conference, Administrative and Editorial Committee/Board (New York, NY: Catholic Book Publishing Co., 1970).

7. Anon., ch. 70, The Cloud of Unknowing, Classic of Medeival Mysticism, Evelyn Underhill, ed., (Minneola, NY: Dover Publications, 2003) p.121. Found online at Googlebooks.com. See http://books.google.com/books?id=BVDGVDaZcsgC&pg=PA121&dq=The+Cloud+of+Unknowing+The+most+goodly+knowing+of+God,+is+that+which+is+known+by+unknowing&hl=en&ei=Y2YPTcXlCoT48Abx0t2aDg&sa=X&oi=book_result&ct=result&resnum=1&ved=0CCoQ6AEwAA#v=onepage&q&f=false.

8. T. S. Eliot, Opening Stanza, Choruses From the Rock, A Guide to the Selected Poems of T. S. Eliot, B. C. Southam, ed., (New York, NY: Houghton Mifflin Harcourt, 1996) p.250. See also Karl Rahner, ed. Encyclopedia of Theology, The Concise Sacramentum Mundi, (New York, NY: Seabury Press, 1975) pp. 801–813.

Chapter Thirty-Two
Consciousness and Unconsciousness

To be conscious is to be critically aware of a reality. It is to perceive or notice with a degree of controlled thought and observation and to experience the reality within one's inner self. Even a carrot has carrot consciousness or a dog has a dog consciousness, but human consciousness is different. We have the potential to know that we know.

In its literal sense, the word "consciousness" means "internal knowledge" or "with awareness."[1] But, it is more than a mental process. In its broadest sense it includes our spirituality, bodily senses, mental thoughts, emotions, feelings, and intuitions. It is the sum total of all phenomena inside us. To quote theologian Bernard Lonergan, "The dynamic state of love of God is conscious without being known, it is an experience of mystery."[2]

Consciousness and spiritual energy can perhaps be seen as synonymous. As we grow in consciousness and become aware of our own and others realities, we begin to experience the collective gathering of life's energy. When, in reality, one sees and experiences the energy of life itself, that becomes consciousness.

The term "self-consciousness" is used to denote the higher state of consciousness where we recognize this state of awareness within us and are able to reflect on it and contemplate it introspectively. Greater consciousness requires one to be silent, turn inward, contemplate and reflect. Teilhard de Chardin, has said, "Life moves to higher and higher levels of consciousness . . . the higher forms of life not only 'know'—we know that we know."[3]

The more we have consciousness of our knowing powers, and how they impact lives within our own reality and others realities, the more we become self-conscious and self-realized. On the other hand, most of the workings of the human body are driven by an unconscious awareness. Functions like breathing, digestion, heartbeat, blinking, etc., are for the most part, operating at an unconscious level, so that our consciousness is free to develop.

We cannot speak too definitively about our unconsciousness (mystery) simply because it is not in our consciousness (reality). When someone or something is in our unconsciousness, it/they are out of our immediate field of awareness or reality. One can be aware of someone or something, but not be fully aware that they are aware. Unconsciousness refers to a level of awareness within our inner self which is either below the level of full awareness (subconsciousness) or there is absolutely no perceived reality. There may be some realization occurring, but we are not conscious of it or aware of it because it is at the level of mystery. It is not yet at the door of our consciousness or within our field of awareness as a reality.

An example here might be someone walking along being aware at some level of their subconscious that there are clouds in the distance, but not really "seeing" them with their full awareness. When another person they are walking with states, "look how beautiful the clouds are today," we then see those clouds at a higher level of our consciousness than we might have previously.

Both consciousness and unconsciousness have access to reality. The two create their own interpretations of reality. With consciousness, there is a "realizing;" with unconsciousness, we are not "realizing." But our unconsciousness has a wider view of reality that includes the recognition of things of a spiritual nature, not realized, identified, or recognized by our consciousness.

We are neither pure matter nor pure spirit. Human nature is a single reality; a union comprising both. Our consciousness helps us to understand the created world as reality around us. Our unconsciousness helps us to fathom that we, as embodied spirits, or spiritized bodies, can mysteriously be aware of someone or something at some level of our humanity. Our unconscious can be speaking to our conscious without our full knowledge or awareness.

When we speak of transcendent reality, we speak of mystery. We are not directly conscious of mystery. So, the God of mystery can be even more active in our unconsciousness than in our consciousness. Because consciousness has something to do with spiritual energy or life's energy, the Holy Spirit (mystery) can "inspire" our spirit and transform our spirit from within (our reality). In doing this what had previously been unconsciousness can move to the level of consciousness.

Growing in consciousness should mean that we will begin to experience the sacramental presence of God in all of created reality; in the world around us, in others, and in ourselves. We will also begin to experience God as uncreated mystery as God gives the grace. As grace is accepted, our consciousness can lead to self-realization and self-transcendence. The higher levels of consciousness include not only reflection, contemplation, and meditation on God as a transcendent reality, but increasing introspective illumination on our innermost reality of being. Consciousness increases awareness of not only Who is God? And Who is Jesus? But also, What is a human being? And Who am I?

Greater consciousness should result in greater awareness of "reality of being." As a spiritual awareness, it should begin to manifest itself, be actualized, and then realized. The evidence that any being is "getting real" is the producing of more fruit of the Spirit in their lives; love, joy, peace, patience, kindness, gentleness, faithfulness, humility, and self-control (Gal 5:22).[4]

We are moving in history as life's collective energy is gathering. We are moving from unconsciousness to consciousness, from consciousness to self-consciousness, from self-consciousness to Christ-consciousness. As we move toward what theologian Teilhard de Chardin called the "Omega Point"[5] and the culmination of history and reality, the mystery of Christ in us will bring greater revelation of that mystery and a Christ-consciousness, as all reality begins to be unified in Christ.

Quoting Teilhard de Chardin, writing about the rise of consciousness: "No reality in the world can go on increasing without sooner or later reaching a critical point involving some change of state."[6]

NOTES

1. "Consciousness." Douglas Harper, ed., Online Etymology Dictionary. Found online at http://www.etymonline.com/index.php?search=conscious&searchmode=none.

2. Bernard Lonergan, Method in Theology, Lonergan Research Institute, ed., (Toronto, Canada: University of Toronto Press, 1990) p. 106.

3. Pierre Teilhard de Chardin, The Phenomenon of Man, Bernard Wall, ed. (New York, NY: Harper and Row Publishing, 1959).

4. Gal 5:22, New American Bible, St. Joseph Edition, Confraternity of Christian Doctrine, Board of Trustees/National Conference of Catholic Bishops/United States Catholic Conference, Administrative and Editorial Committee/Board (New York, NY: Catholic Book Publishing Co., 1970).

5. Pierre Teilhard de Chardin, The Phenomenon of Man, Bernard Wall, ed.(New York, NY: Harper and Row Publishing, 1959) pp. 57, 257–264, 268–272, 288, 291–298, 307–309.

6. Pierre Teilhard de Chardin, The Phenomenon of Man, The Rise of Consciousness, ch. 3, Bernard Wall, ed.(New York, NY: Harper and Row Publishing, 1959) p. 152.

Chapter Thirty-Three

Humanity and Divinity: The Cross +

The symbol of the cross is found carved in many of the early Christian catacombs. But, as a symbol, the cross predates Christianity and is found in many ancient cultures. It was even discovered among archeological finds of the neolithic age. The Egyptian ankh, for example, resembles the cross, as do the symbols of many peoples, including the earlier Chaldean (Babylonian) and Phoenician (Canaanite) cultures.[1] It should be noted, however, that no mention of the cross as a symbol is made throughout the books of the Old Testament or in the broader body of ancient Hebrew literature. Its basis did not seem to have any Judaic roots. But in many of the other ancient cultures, the cross had universal acceptance and significance as a sacred symbol particularly for nature worship or worship of the sun.[2]

The crucifixion of Jesus was a historical reality and the cross a great mystery that the early Christian church had to grapple with and reconcile (1 Cor 1:23). After all, a suffering, crucified messiah was something that was foreign to the Judaism of that day. In addition to the historical significance of the cross as the wooden structure on which Jesus died, or the crucifix, the cross in and of itself possessed symbolic value. It is a mysterious symbol which in no way diminishes the historical reality. As such, there does seem to exist a correspondence in the layers of meaning and mystery it reveals, as it was the intersection where humanity met divinity.

In speaking of "the cross," the New Testament is most often referring symbolically to the sacrifice and redemptive work of Jesus and not the literal wood on which he was crucified. The cross of Christ became a symbol, early on, which brought together many fundamental Christian concepts and ideas such as Christ's saving work and Christ's victory over sin and death (1 Cor 1:17; Gal 2:19, 6:14; Eph 2:16; Phil 3:18).[3] Like any symbol, its function was first to remind us of something else and then point the way for us, as human beings, to that something.

According to Carl Jung, a symbol should not have any definition, but many levels of meaning. It should represent something whose meaning is difficult to grasp intellectually in its full scope. Similar to a work of art, it should defy any simple description which is free of nuance. If you can define it, then it is no longer a symbol, but a sign.[4]

A symbol, is certainly first a sign, however, it can also be distinguished from a sign by being more adequate in its aptness. The sign merely points to something else, but the symbol is closer to the reality of the thing signified and indicates a special quality and meaningfulness. But this distinction also seems to indicate the limitation, ambiguity, and mystery inherent in the symbol. At the cross of Christ, reality meets mystery and humanity meets divinity, as God takes on the flesh, blood, and bone of a human. Jesus then becomes for us, the human face of God.

A symbol points to and communicates the reality which lies behind it. But, it is also a sign that is so very intimately connected with the reality that it essentially embodies what it signifies. It is often a vehicle of the sacred and mysterious. In this particular sense, the cross of Jesus Christ can be called the personal symbol of Jesus Christ. For Christians, it is Jesus who makes the universality of the cross, a most personal symbol of reality for him and for us. Only at the end of history will the cross of Jesus Christ be seen as a personal reality for all of creation universally, as all creation intersects at the center of the cross and converges to the "Omega Point."[5]

The cross has become the symbol of the Christian mystery in which all reality is centered in Christ. All reality can therefore be called, Christocentric. In the cross, all things are brought together and reunited with God (Col 1: 15–20).[6] Through the cross, Jesus becomes the center of all reality of being; the mid-point, not only between reality and mystery, but between God and man, eternity and history, divinity and humanity, heaven and earth, good and evil etc. He becomes at one and the same time, a universal reality and personal mystery; a personal reality and a mystery of cosmic proportion.

At the cross, all vertical lines of mystery, in a descent from above and ascent from below, meet with the horizontal lines of intelligible reality at the center. At the center of the cross is Christ. At that center, all duality of the vertical and horizontal, no longer exist in their dualism, they intersect, meet, and are unified. The vertical and horizontal lines disappear in the oneness of the cross. There is a unity of opposites as God becomes man and man becomes God. In the ensuing resurrection, reality is once more swallowed up by mystery.

At the center, the gateway to eternity is opened and at the horizontal and the vertical intersection, the four lines meet. Here all worldly realities; elements of earth, wind, water, and fire, merge and meet. All human realities, seen in terms of mind, body, soul, or spirit, merge and meet. The dying and rising seen in nature in the four seasons of summer, fall, winter, and spring meet at the center and yield to what has become the single most ultimate act of all dying and rising. All spatial directions, north, south, east, and west, and all past, present, future, and eternal realities converge at the center of time and eternity. The cross of Christ becomes the center of all reality of being, both human being and supreme being. Each of the four lines becomes a radius; and as such, they radiate. As they radiate, they permeate every being in all of history and eternity, transforming history into salvation history and bringing about the possibility of eternal salvation.

Even the human body with outstretched arms makes the symbol of the cross. And Roman Catholics bless themselves in memory of the cross of Jesus Christ. They make the sign of the cross by touching forehead, breast, and then in sequence, the left and right shoulders.

Following the crucifixion, the reality of the cross became a mystery which is actualized in human persons. In human beings, the cross is made real through the resurrected Jesus and the dynamic presence of the Holy Spirit. It is the Holy Spirit who continues the process of self-actualization in humanity begun by Jesus. Self-actualization in human beings can potentially become self-realization.

The end of history will bring an end to reality as we know it and then all actualization will ultimately give way to the realization of Christ at the "Omega Point."[7] That this is occurring in the present is the hope of a future reality. How it is occurring in the present is an ongoing mystery hidden with the resurrected Christ and the yet deeper layers of meaning of the symbol of the cross of Christ.

Ultimately for us, to be fully human is to be fully divine. If we know that we are not fully divine, then we cannot as yet even call ourselves fully human. We can only be called "pre-human" or a "human becoming" as contrasted with what truly would one day be for us the experience of a "human being."

NOTES

1. "The Ankh/Other Symbols." Signs of Life: A Pictorial Dictionary of Symbols, H. M. Raphaellian, Felix Marti-Ibanez, ed., (Whitefish, MT: Kessinger Publishing, 2006) p. 24. Found online at Googlebooks.com. See the Googlebooks website at http://books.google.com/books?id=jqHqGCgIeWAC&pg=PA24&dq=the+ankh&hl=

en&ei=EI0QTZaWOYGC8gbOjaXmAQ&sa=X&oi=book_result&ct=result&resnum=10&ved=0CE8Q6AEwCQ#v=onepage&q=the%20ankh&f=false.

2. Jerome Biblical Commentary, Raymond E. Brown, S.S., Joseph Fitzmeyer, S.J., Roland Murphy, O. Carm., ed., (Englewood Cliffs, NJ: Prentice Hall Publishing, 1968) Sec. 51:19–64:28.

3. 1 Cor 1:23; 1 Cor 1:17; Gal 2:19, 6:14; Eph 2:16; Phil 3:18, New American Bible, St. Joseph Edition, Confraternity of Christian Doctrine, Board of Trustees/National Conference of Catholic Bishops/United States Catholic Conference, Administrative and Editorial Committee/Board (New York, NY: Catholic Book Publishing Co., 1970).

4. Carl Jung, Man and His Symbols, Marie Luise Von Franz, John Freeman, ed., (New York, NY: Random House/Dell Publishing, 1968).

5. "Omega Point." Pierre Teilhard de Chardin, The Phenomenon of Man, Bernard Wall, ed.(New York, NY: Harper and Row Publishing, 1959) pp. 57, 257–264, 268–272, 288, 291–298, 307–309.

6. Col 1: 15–20, New American Bible, St. Joseph Edition, Confraternity of Christian Doctrine, Board of Trustees/National Conference of Catholic Bishops/United States Catholic Conference, Administrative and Editorial Committee/Board (New York, NY: Catholic Book Publishing Co., 1970).

7. "Omega Point." Pierre Teilhard de Chardin, The Phenomenon of Man, Bernard Wall, ed.(New York, NY: Harper and Row Publishing, 1959) pp. 57, 257–264, 268–272, 288, 291–298, 307–309.

Chapter Thirty-Four

Man the Reality and God the Mystery

God is other, has no borders, and is The Eternal "You." Every "you" is but a glimpse into the mystery of The Eternal "You." When I encounter or am encountered by any "you," I encounter God. Essentially, I become an "I" through many "yous."

One dimension of this God is mystery so incredibly awesome in its brightness that if we look directly into the face of God, we are blinded. Because of this, we picture this God of mystery as dwelling far away, hidden by clouds, and dwelling beyond the heavens (1 Tim. 6:16). Yet, this same God dwells very near to us and is present in our midst in Jesus Christ. That in itself is also a mystery. We are told in the Gospel of John ch.1 vs.18, "No one has ever seen God. The only Son, God who is at the Father's side, has revealed him."[1]

Karl Rahner, S.J., has been recognized as one of the leading theologians of the twentieth century. To Rahner, God is best described as "Holy Mystery." This Holy Mystery is always present to the world and persons in the world. Because we are at one and the same time both human beings and human becomings, our relationship with this Holy Mystery is a process of self-transcendence. Therefore, all theology for Rahner, becomes "Transcendental Anthropology."

The Holy Mystery, which is God, became Rahner's theological touchstone. He envisioned the mystery to be not only a description of God, but also the very nature of human consciousness. Following on Martin Heidegger's philosophy, Rahner would say that.: "The human being is a questioning being because the person himself is a question."[2] And he maintained further that the questioning nature of the human person guaranteed that mystery would remain an intrinsic part of human knowing. Rahner is therefore able to argue that the mystery of God and the mystery of the human spirit are in continuity.

God, as Holy Mystery, is the One to whom all of reality and all of history are oriented. Any human person is self-transcendent to the extent that they are oriented beyond themselves and toward the mystery. God is already present within the human person to give the grace to bring the reality of our humanity, at our point in history, into the mystery.

Without facing the reality that our lives are shrouded in mystery, any openness to revelation will inevitably be closed off. Revelation cannot really mean an "unveiling" for us, unless we already have at least some propensity and access to the depth of the mystery that it reveals. So, we are by our very nature already open to the Holy Mystery as we self-transcend.

But, "Transcendental Anthropology" is termed as such because theological propositions rarely deal with the Divine in and of itself, but with God in relation to human beings and human existence. We cannot discuss matter and spirit or nature and grace, for example, without discussing God and man. So, any kind of theology should have an anthropological dimension. The question is not . . . "Does theology relate to anthropology?" Because it can't help doing so. The question really becomes . . . "What kind of a relation does it have?"[3]

As Christians, we interpret both God and human existence in light of our faith in Jesus Christ. So, whatever we have to say about the ultimate meaning of human existence is something said, at the same time, about Jesus Christ and about God. And whatever we say about God and Jesus Christ is something we are saying about ourselves and our human existence.

How can we accept as truths, what is revealed by God in scripture and Christian Tradition, unless we apply them to understanding who we are in reality? And further, what is the meaning, direction, purpose, and ultimate destiny of our lives? If we believe that only in Christ can we come to a full understanding of who we are and of our final destiny beyond this world's reality, then we will orient ourselves to the God of mystery.

The basis of Christian human existence is the realizable and realizing experience of new union with God in Christ. This is an ontological reality/spiritual mystery and cannot be perceived by our consciousness. In faith then, we can only reconcile our spirit with the ontological reality being "realized" within us and orient ourselves to the spiritual mystery.

But, as human beings, we are not detached observers of either reality or mystery. We are simultaneously the subject and the object of the inquiry, "Who is God? Who is Jesus Christ? Who am I?" This is one interrelated question which addresses our reality of being and is at the heart of our "getting real."

As Christians we profess that through the death and resurrection of Jesus Christ, the beyond is really in our midst. And that God is mysteriously present to us in the Spirit. But, the above question needs to be addressed even by those who do not believe that their human existence and reality has any connection to Jesus Christ and the mystery of God. The conclusions may be different, however, the question is always being addressed because man him/herself is the question.

In no other being was the mystery of God more fully realized than in Jesus Christ, who became God for us and then God in us through the power of the Holy Spirit. In part, God's reality is to be the Holy Mystery in us as well. The Holy Mystery in us has become part of man's reality.

NOTES

1. 1 Tim. 6:16; Jn 1: 18, New American Bible, St. Joseph Edition, Conf. of Christian Doctrine, Board of Trustees/National Conference of Catholic Bishops/United States Catholic Conference, Administrative and Editorial Committee/Board (New York, NY: Catholic Book Publishing Co., 1970).

2. "Essence." Encyclopedia of Theology, The Concise Sacramentum Mundi, Karl Rahner ed., (New York, NY: Seabury/Crossroads Press, 1975) p. 440. See also Questions and Questioning, Michael Meyer, ed., (New York, NY: Walter de Gruyter Publishing, 1988).

3. "Transcendental Anthropology." in Richard P. McBrien, ed., Catholicism: Study Edition (Minneapolis, MN: Winston Press, 1981 and New York, NY: Harper Collins Publishers, 1994) pp. 128–134, 186, 193–194, 222–223, 250, 319, 498, 642–647, 956. See also Karl Rahner, Foundations of Christian Faith, An Introduction to the Idea of Christianity, Karl Rahner, ed. (New York, NY: Crossroads Publishing, 1989) and Karl Rahner: Theology and Philosophy, Karen Kilby, ed., (New York, NY: Routledge & Co./Taylor & Francis Group, 2004) p. 32.

Chapter Thirty-Five

God the Reality and Man the Mystery

God's reality is to be Spirit; the Holy Spirit. Spirit is between "I" and "You" and spirituality comes to life in the Spirit. Theology comes to life in language. After all, theology is what has been called, a "God-language." If theology is to speak about God, it cannot really be put into relevant words without a background of silence out of which the Spirit and the words will come. One must first be speaking to God and listening to God. Otherwise, how can there be any words at all to discuss something like a transcendent reality?

Whether we use the term "mystery" or the term "transcendent reality," we are simply using different words to say the same thing about God and God's reality. The two terms are synonymous.

God is both the origin and goal of all reality. The word, "God," in our language, often appears as if God is a being who is known. But a transcendent reality refers to One who is both unknowable and unknown. So even the word, "God," is an ambiguous word. Although the scriptures encourage us to seek God for our benefit; in reality, any seeking of God will lead us into God, the transcendent Reality, because there is nothing or no one in which God cannot be found. But, God will always be more than who and what we find.

God is beyond, above, and beneath all names, forms, definitions, and categories and simultaneously within all created, ordinary, tangible, visible, immediately available, and concrete reality. God is the primordial ground of all reality and the One to whom all reality is "being oriented." Because God IS Being. We, as human beings, have no possible way that we can fully see God objectively as "Being in Reality."

God transcends anything and everything we could think or say about God in our reality. Because of this, there is nothing that we can say about God as a reality that doesn't end up being something said about our human nature and human existence. For example, when we say, "God spoke to me," we make the assumption that God has a mouth like us and uses words to communicate. Therefore, only in Jesus Christ is God "realized" so that God can be "realizable" for us as human beings.[1]

So, God's reality is impossible to discuss definitively because of God's ineffable character. Therefore, in the end we will always be talking about our mystery and ultimately be rendered once again to silence. On the other hand, scripture does indicate mystical and spiritual experiences of God as a transcendent reality, especially in Apocalyptic literature. Only an intervention by God in the Spirit can lift man out of our human reality to allow for a mystical and ecstatic experience of God in our spirit as a transcendent reality (see Rev. 1:10; 17:3; 21:10).[2] And at the same time that God is revealing Godself, God is concealing Godself. We can never experience the transcendent reality who is God all at once.

As was discussed previously, everything in the field of time and space is dual; man-woman, truth-untruth, good-evil, light-dark, etc. Duality is our human experience of reality. But beyond the duality is a singularity, a oneness. God has revealed to us that God's reality is to be OneGod in three persons. Not that we can ever understand that Absolute Mystery of the Holy Trinity, but when we go beyond duality, there we enter transcendent reality. God, as a transcendent reality, can only be contemplated as a mystery within the mind and heart of man, who is him/herself a mystery.

One of the greatest evidences for the existence of God as transcendent reality is our own process of self-actualization, self-realization, and self-transcendence. No matter where we are on our journey, we still know less about Who am I? than we know. That question, as stated earlier is intrinsically interwoven with the questions, Who is Jesus Christ? And Who is God? These three questions really become one. To ask oneself or be asked, Who are you? Is really asking, What is your reality? And the reality of the Christian life is a contemplative life centered on that which is mysterious, divine, heavenly, spiritual, eternal, supernatural, universal, filled with grace, and more consciously focused on knowing God, Jesus, and one's true self.

As Christians, the God/Jesus/me? question must ultimately await the moment of our own experience of resurrection from the dead. But the fact that they exist as one mysterious question within the deepest recesses of man's humanity indicates that there is an answer to the question which lies somewhere in there/out there in the totality of all reality. Because even though we as human persons don't know the complete answer to the one mysterious question, we certainly know the question exists in us as a question which concerns our essence as well as our existence in reality. This one question is at the heart of what it will mean for us to "Get Real."

NOTES

1. Transcendence." in Richard P. McBrien, ed., Catholicism: Study Edition (Minneapolis, MN: Winston Press, 1981 and New York, NY: Harper Collins Publishers, 1994) pp. 193–194, 222–223, 498.

2. Rev. 1:10; 17:3; 21:10, New American Bible, St. Joseph Edition, Conf. of Christian Doctrine, Board of Trustees/National Conf. of Catholic Bishops/U.S. Catholic Conf., Admin. and Editorial Committee/Board (New York, NY: Catholic Book Pub. Co., 1970).

Chapter Thirty-Six

Self-Transcending

Maslow's *Hierarchy of Needs* is a theory in Psychology proposed by Abraham Maslow in the 1940's. It is presented in the form of a pyramid. At the base are "physiological needs," such as breathing, food, water etc. Above those basic needs are a need for "safety," then a need for "love and belonging." Near the top of the pyramid is the need for "self esteem." As a psychological theory, the highest achievement in Maslow's *Hierarchy of Needs*, at one time, was "Self-Actualization" (development of one's maximum potential and capacities). Self-Actualization was seen as the highest need which could potentially be "realized" after all the lower level needs were met.[1]

However, near the end of Maslow's life (1970), he revealed that he believed that there was a higher level above Self-Actualization (theory Y) and that was "Self-Transcendence" (theory Z). He stated that Self-Transcenders were "more aware of the realm of being" and that they "saw sacredness in all things." He understood Self-Transcendence to be a "spiritual awakening and liberation from egocentricity."[2]

I believe that self-transcending should be discussed beyond the level of any psychological theory and we have the potential as human persons to show its basis as a theological principle. Certainly Karl Rahner, one of the foremost theologians of this century, maintained that self-transcendence was a dimension of his Theological Anthropology.[3]

God, the Holy Mystery and Transcendent Reality, is present to persons in the world as the principle of their self-transcending. Because we are made in the image and likeness of God, our authenticity in reality consists in our being loving and good like God. Therefore, we enter into the authenticity and genuineness of transcendent reality through our capacity for self-transcending.

It is the mysterious capacity within the human to become a higher being while remaining at all times, thoroughly human. Through the movement and acceptance of grace, and orientation to the transcendent ground of all reality, who is the God of mystery, humans can begin to realize their greater potential. As humans, we have the capacity within us to move beyond ourselves and to become something higher or better than who we are now. This is not to say that we become something other than human, or we become God, but only that we are indeed becoming human as God intended. Self-transcending will inevitably create a tension within the self, however, because there will often exist a tension between the self as transcending and the self as transcended.

The Reign of God, we are told, is "already in our midst (Lk 17:21),"[4] so the above and beyond is already present to us as the ground of reality and the ground of our being. Theologians such as, Teilhard de Chardin and Karl Rahner have argued that the whole of the historical process is in dynamic movement from lower to higher, from unconsciousness to consciousness, and from consciousness to self-consciousness. Both history and humanity includes us. We are constantly in a state of "becoming."[5]

With the incarnation of Jesus Christ, history has been set in motion to head to its end point where all things in reality will be unified mysteriously in Christ. The whole movement of matter in the universe is ultimately directed toward spirit and the whole movement of spirit is directed toward Christ in unity. So, we are not only moving from matter to spirit, but also from lower to higher and unconsciousness to consciousness. In our self-transcending, we are also moving from consciousness to self-consciousness and from self-consciousness, ultimately to Christ-consciousness.

As has been stated previously, when we experience the mystery of self-transcending we are not only human beings, we are essentially human becomings, or if you prefer, we are now pre-human and becoming a human being. Jesus Christ's entrance into history was the highest point of a human becoming and the greatest moment of any self-transcendence. But, history is continuing on its course toward its conclusion and the question becomes "What are we doing at our moment in history?"

Quoting theologian Bernard Lonergan: "It is finally, only by reaching the sustained self-transcendence of the virtuous man that one becomes a good judge, not on this or that human act, but on the whole range of human goodness."[6]

Given the acceptance of grace, our capacity to love and to be loved; then moving from smaller to deeper questions concerning reality, God, Christ, humanity, and the true self, constitutes our capacity for self-transcendence.

Quoting Karl Rahner: "The essence of any being whose self-transcendence is in question does not determine the limits of what can be produced in the advance beyond itself. It can, however, be an indication, that from some definite limited potentiality something is coming to be and must come about that is not yet a reality."[7]

Self-transcending, not only allows us to go above and beyond our self in reality, it encounters the God of mystery who is wholly other and independent of our self; the Eternal "You." This relates particularly to spiritual experience, because in its orientation and direction to God, the Holy Mystery, the spirit within the human person is oriented and directed to the Absolute Being and Ultimate Reality; the primordial ground of our reality of being; who is Spirit; The Holy Spirit.

NOTES

1. Abraham Maslow, Hierarchy of Needs, (London, UK: Institute of Management, 1998). See also Abraham Maslow, Maslow's Hierarchy of Needs, Frederic Miller, Agnes Vandome, John McBrewster, ed., (Beau Bassin, Maur.: Alphascript Publishing/VDM Publishing House, 2010).
2. "Self-Transcendence." Abraham Maslow, Transpersonal Psychology and Self-Transcendence, found online at http://www.abrahammaslow.com/m_motivation/Transpersonal_Psychology.asp See also "Self-Transcendence" Abraham Maslow, Self-Actualization and the Radical Gospel, Louis Roy, ed., (Collegeville, MN: Liturgical Press, 2010) p. 19. Found online at Googlebooks.com. See website http://books.google.com/books?id=81dowWciukUC&pg=PA19&dq=abraham+maslow+self+transcendence&hl=en&ei=r6MQTcrJGsG78gaUjK2LAQ&sa=X&oi=book_result&ct=result&resnum=1&ved=0CCYQ6AEwAA#v=onepage&q=abraham%20maslow%20self%20transcendence&f=false.
3. "Self-Transcendence." Encyclopedia of Theology, The Concise Sacramentum Mundi, Karl Rahner ed., (New York, NY: Seabury/Crossroads Press, 1975) p. 698. See also Karl Rahner, Foundations of Christian Faith, An Introduction to the Idea of Christianity, Karl Rahner, ed. (New York, NY: Seabury/Crossroads Publishing, 1989) p. 225.
4. Lk 17:21, New American Bible, St. Joseph Edition, Confraternity of Christian Doctrine, Board of Trustees/National Conference of Catholic Bishops/United States Catholic Conference, Administrative and Editorial Committee/Board (New York, NY: Catholic Book Publishing Co., 1970).
5. Teilhard de Chardin, Divine Mileau, (New York, NY: HarperCollins Publishing, 1960). See also Catholicism, New Study Edition, Richard McBrien, ed., (New York, NY: HarperCollins Publishers, 1994) p. 496. Found online at googlebooks.com. See the Googlebooks website at http://books.google.com/books?id=cldKKwvF284C&pg=PA496&dq=de+chardin+lower+to+higher+and+from+unconsciousness+to+consciousness.&hl=en&ei=1rIQTf2tKMP38AaI8In9DQ&sa=X&oi=book_result&ct=result&resnum=1&ved=0CCMQ6AEwAA#v=onepage&q=de%20chardin%20lower%20to%20higher%20and%20from%20unconsciousness%20to%20consciousness.&f=false.
6. Bernard Lonergan, Method in Theology, ch. 2, Lonergan Research Institute, ed., (Toronto, Canada: University of Toronto Press, 1990) p. 35.
7. Karl Rahner, Hominization, The Evolutionary Origin of Man as a Theological Problem, W. T. O'Hara, ed., (New York, NY: Herder & Herder, 1965) Sec. 3.

Chapter Thirty-Seven

Conclusion: God Mysteriously in Us and Us Really in God

As Christians we are called "the temple of the Holy Spirit" because the Holy Spirit continues to proceed from the Lord of the Spirit, Jesus Christ, sent by the Father. He has become through His dying and rising a life-giving Spirit for us and within us. Scripture tells us, "Do you not know that you are the temple of God and that the Spirit of God dwells in you? (1 Cor 3:16)" and "We are the temple of the living God (2 Cor 6:16)," as well as "In Him you also are being built together into a dwelling place for God in the Spirit (EPH 2:22)."

To believe in the Holy Spirit is first, to profess that the Holy Spirit is one of the distinct persons of the Trinity; co-natural and consubstantial with the Father and the Son. The Holy Spirit has been at work with the Father and the Son from the beginning. The redeeming incarnation of the Son revealed and gave the Holy Spirit which proceeds from the Father and the Son. In this, our modern age, history is continuing to move to its end point.

If the mystery of the Holy Spirit of God is now being "realized" within us, our lives should be manifesting the "Fruit of the Spirit, in love, joy, peace, patience, kindness, gentleness, faithfulness, humility, and self-control (Gal 5:22)."[1] If we have welcomed and received the One whom the Father has sent into our hearts, we have received the Spirit of His Son, the Holy Spirit. Receiving the Holy Spirit implies that we have received the Father and Son as well. They are distinct, but inseparable.

Therefore, God is mysteriously in us. That should not translate to God is us. God is in us, but God remains Wholly Other and Holy Other. Grace supposes the nature of the human person. Conversely, our human nature supposes the grace. So, grace is not an add-on to our human nature.[2] The Holy Spirit of God dwelling in us as temples of God can transform us from within and orient us toward God. Here, God's offer of grace proceeds to be "actualized" and then ultimately, "realized" as we personally experience the actualization of grace. No other finite reality can be a substitute for the spiritual reality that is occurring when we encounter the Holy Spirit of God within us. For, when we encounter the Holy Spirit in us, we encounter the very life-breath of God, the Spirit of the Logos, the Spirit of the Word. This will begin to create an awareness that God is not only mysteriously in us, but also that we are really in God.

Herein lies one of the most exciting of all "GET REAL" experiences, as personal reality meets the absolute mystery of the Triune God within. Ultimately then, the duality of reality and mystery will end. We will know that mystery will eventually become the home of our reality. As has been said by others before, history has always been and will forever be "His-story." But, for us, mystery will also then become the revealing of "my-story" as well.

And finally, until we actually "GET REAL," we must be satisfied for now just simply to find the time and space at our moment in history to enter into the mystery and . . .

"GET SILENCE."

NOTES

1. 1 Cor 3:16; 2 Cor 6:16; EPH 2:22; Gal 5:22, New American Bible, St. Joseph Edition, Confraternity of Christian Doctrine, Board of Trustees/National Conference of Catholic Bishops/United States Catholic Conference, Administrative and Editorial Committee/Board (New York, NY: Catholic Book Publishing Co., 1970).

2. "Nature" and "Grace," Catholic Encyclopedia, From the New Advent Encyclopedia, found on the New Advent CD-ROM by Kevin Knight (Denver, CO: Advent International, 2009). See also the New Advent website at http://www.newadvent.org/fathers/1503.htm And for Thomas Aquinas, Summa, see Questions 109 and 113, New Advent Website at http://www.newadvent.org/summa/2109.htmand http://www.newadvent.org/summa/2113.htm See also "Nature and Grace" in Richard P. McBrien, ed., Catholicism: Study Edition (Minneapolis, MN: Winston Press, 1981 and New York, NY: HarperCollins Publishers, 1994) pp. 129, 134, 146, 151–167, 225–226, 298, 309, 324–325, 463, 753, 910–911, 1068, 1120–1121, 1128–1133, 1174, 1183.

Index

Abercius, 43–45
absolute mystery, 92–94, 107–8
acolytes, 40–41, 68–73
actual, 3–8
actuality, 3–8
Adonai/My Lord, 59–65
Analogy, 92–94
Ankh, 138–40
Anselm, 87–90
apocalypse/apocalypticism, 37–38, 50–54, 68–73, 145–46
Apocalypse of John, 50–54, 68–73, 98–102
apocrypha, 98–102
Aquinas, Thomas, 3–8, 10–12, 25–28, 47–54, 87–90, 111–13, 118–19, 121–22, 125–26, 128–29, 131–33
Aristotle, 3–8, 10–12, 18–19, 40–41, 121–22, 128–29
Ark of the Covenant, 50–54
Augustine, 10–12, 92–94, 118–19, 128–29
authenticity, 3–8
Averroes, 3–8

Baptism, rite of, 47–48
becoming, 3–8
beginning and end times, 98–102

being, 3–8
belief, 10–12
Berger, Peter, 121–22
bias, 10–12, 14–17
Bible, The: as authoritative, 10–12; as revelation, 50–54; and myth, 55–57; and historical criticism, 50–57; and the Old Testament, 59–65; and the New Testament, 68–73; and suffering, 75–76; and miracles, 78–81
bliss, 125–26
Boethius, 111–13, 118–19, 128–29
Book of Revelation. *See* Apocalypse of John
breathing, 115–17
Buddhism, 107–8

Campbell, Joseph, 55–57, 107–8
character, 10–12
Chardin, Teilhard de, 10–13, 20–23, 87–90, 111–13, 115–17, 128–29, 131–33, 135–37, 148–50
Choruses From the Rock, 131–33
Christ-consciousness. *See* consciousness
Chungste, 107–8
Cloud of Unknowing, 131–33
comedy and tragedy, 121–22

Index

consciousness, 14–17, 55–57, 75–76, 87–90, 95–96, 111–13, 115–17, 131–33, 135–37, 142–44, 148–50
Constantine the Emperor, 43–45
contemplative prayer, 131–33, 135–37, 145–46
creation, 14–17, 59–65, 68–73, 95–96
cross of Christ, 138–40
crucifixion, 75–76, 138–40
cult of Isis, 40–41, 59–65

Daniel, Book of, 59–65, 68–73, 98–102
death, 20–23, 40–41, 50–54, 59–65, 68–73, 78–81, 115–17, 125–26, 128–29, 138–40, 142–44, 151–52
Demeter, 40–41
destiny, 20–23, 142–44
Dionysus, 40–41
Discipline of the Secret, 43–45
divinity, 138–40
dreams, 55–57, 59–65, 68–73
duality, 107–8, 111–13, 115–17, 118–19, 125–26, 138–40, 145–46, 151–52

early Christianity, 43–45, 68–73
earth, 125–26, 128–29
Einstein, Albert, 115–17
El/El Shaddai, 59–65
Eliot, T.S., 131–33
elohim, 59–65
energy, 115–17, 121–22, 135–37
error, 10–12
essence, 3–8, 14–17, 25–28, 87–90, 92–94, 115–17, 121–22, 131–33
eternity, 128–29, 138–40, 142–44, 145–46, 148–50
eucharist, 47–48
Eve, 95–96
existence, 3–8, 14–17, 25–28, 87–90, 115–17, 121–22, 142–44, 145–46

faith, 10–12, 25–28, 37–38, 50–54, 68–73, 87–90, 142–44
falsity, 10–12
fate, 20–23

Fathers of the early church, 43–45, 87–90, 98–102, 118–19
female, 95–96
finality, 20–23
fish symbol, 43–45
Francis of Assisi, 47–48
free-will, 20–23, 30–33, 118–19, 128–29
fruit of the Spirit, 30–33, 87–90, 128–29, 135–37, 151–52

genuineness, 3–8
Get Real, vi, 25–28, 30–33, 87–90, 135–37, 142–44, 145–46, 151–52
Globe, 125–26
God, 3–8, 10–12, 14–17, 25–28, 30–33, 37–38, 47–57, 59–65, 68–73, 75–76, 82–83, 87–90, 92–94, 95–96, 98–102, 107–8, 111–13, 115–17, 118–19, 121–22, 125–26, 128–29, 131–33, 135–37, 138–40, 142–44, 145–46, 148–50, 151–52
goodness, 121–22, 131–33, 138–40, 148–50
grace, 10–12, 14–17, 30–33, 37–38, 47–54, 87–90, 115–17, 118–19, 121–22, 135–37, 142–44, 145–46, 148–50, 51–52

Hamlet, 3–8
heaven, 125–26, 128–29
Heidegger, Martin, 142–44
Heraclitus, 107–8
Hermeneutic Circle, 87–90
Hierarchy of Needs, 148–50
Holy of Holies, 50–54
Holy Mystery, 142–44, 148–50
Holy Spirit, 30–33, 47–54, 68–73, 75–76, 78–81, 87–90, 92–94, 111–13, 115–17, 121–22, 131–33, 135–37, 138–40, 142–44, 145–46, 148–50, 151–52
hominization, 14–17
honesty, 10–12
honor, 10–12

hope, 18–19, 25–28, 68–73
humanity, 138–40, 142–44, 145–46, 148–50, 151–52
humor, 121–22

Ichtus, 43–45
idea, 3–8, 18–19
ideal, 3–8
ignorance, 14–17
imagination, 18–19
incarnation. *See* Jesus Christ
information/Information Age, 131–33
inner realities, 10–12, 135–37, 151–52
integrity, 10–12
Isis, 40–41, 43–45, 59–65
Islam, 98–102

Jehovah, 59–65
Jehovahs Witnesses, 98–102
Jesus Christ, 10–12, 14–17, 20–23, 30–33, 37–38, 43–45, 47–54, 59–65, 68–73, 75–76, 78–81, 82–83, 85–86, 87–90, 92–94, 98–102, 111–13, 115–17, 118–19, 121–22, 125–26, 128–29, 131–33, 135–37, 138–40, 142–44, 145–46, 148–50, 151–52
Joseph the Patriarch, 59–65
judgement, 98–102
judgements and beliefs, 3–8, 10–12
Jung, Carl, 138–40
justice, 10–12

Kingdom of God/Reign of God, 50–54, 68–73, 78–81, 82–83, 85–86, 98–102, 125–26, 148–50
Kingdom of Heaven, 82–83, 125–26, 128–29
"Know Thyself." *See* Oracle at Delphi
knowing/knowledge, 10–12, 14–17, 25–28, 30–33, 37–38, 95–96, 131–33, 135–37, 142–44
kyrios, 59–65

Lady Wisdom, 59–65
Laotse, 107–8

lies, 10–12
life, 14–17
Logos, 14–17, 59–65, 68–73, 151–52
logic, 55–57, 87–90, 92–94, 131–33
Lonergan, Bernard, 135–37, 148–50
love 10–12, 14–17, 25–28, 30–33, 82–83, 87–90, 121–22, 128–29, 131–33, 135–37, 148–50, 151–52

Maslow, Abraham, 148–50
matrimony, 47–48, 55–57, 95–96
matter, 3–8, 95–96, 115–17, 121–22, 135–37, 142–44, 148–50
mediation, 47–54, 75–76, 87–90, 95–96
Mercy Seat, 50–54
Metaphysical Disputations of Suarez, 3–8
Metaphysics of Aristotle, 3–8
Michael/The Archangel Michael, 68–73, 98–102
miracles, 78–81, 85–86
Mormons, 98–102
Moses, 50–54, 59–65, 98–102
Moses Maimonides, 3–8
Museum of the Lateran Basilica, 43–45
mystery: as the Home of Reality, vii-viii; Mystery, definition, 37–38; Mystery, cults & religions, 40–41; and sacramentality, 47–48; and revelation, 50–54; and myth, 55–57; and the Old Testament, 59–65; and the New Testament, 68–73; and suffering, 75–76; and miracles, 78–81; and the Kingdom of God, 82–83; and parables, 85–86; and theology, 87–90; and spiritual experience, 87–90; and mysticism, 87–90; and types of theological mysteries, 92–94; and the female, 95–96; and the Archangel Michael, 98–102; and names, 98–102; and the unity of opposites, 107–8; and the personal and universal, 111–13; and matter and spirit, 115–17; and nature and grace, 118–19; and the natural

and supernatural, 121–22; and heaven and earth, 125–26; and time and eternity, 128–29; and knowing and unknowing, 131–33; and consciousness and unconsciousness, 135–37; and humanity and divinity, 138–40; and the cross of Christ, 138–40; and God, 142–44; and man, 145–46; and self-transcending, 148–50; and conclusions, 151–52
mystery cults, 40–41, 43–45, 68–73
mystery fish, 43–45
mystery religions, 40–41, 43–45
mysticism, 87–90, 145–46
myth, 55–57, 68–73

names, 59–65, 68–73, 98–102
natural and supernatural, 121–22
nature, 47–48, 78–81, 92–94, 95–96, 111–13, 118–19, 121–22, 142–44, 151–52
Nero, the emperor, 43–45, 68–73
new covenant, 98–102
New Testament, 68–73
Nouwen, Henri, 111–13
numbers/numerology, 68–73

old covenant, 98–102
Old Testament, 59–65
Omega Point, 20–23, 30–33, 128–29, 135–37, 138–40
ontology, 3–8
openness, 14–17
Oracle at Delphi, 111–13
Osiris, 40–41

parables, 68–73, 82–83, 85–86
Pascal, Blaise, 50–54
Paul the Apostle, 10–12, 43–45, 50–54, 68–73
Persephone, 40–41
person, 111–13
personal and universal, 111–13, 138–40
Peter, 43–45

Plato, 3–8, 40–41
Plutarch, 40–41
poetry, 55–57, 68–73
power, 78–81
pre-existence, 14–17
prejudice, 10–12, 14–17
prophecy/prophets, 59–65
providence, 78–81
Pythagoras, 40–41

Questioning/Questions, 37–38, 87–90, 111–13, 131–33, 142–44, 145–46, 148–50

Ra, 40–41
Rahner, Karl, 3–8, 20–23, 30–33, 115–17, 121–22, 131–33, 142–44, 148–50
real, def., 3–8
reality: etymology of, vi; reality television shows, vi-viii; reality, defined, 3–8; reality, mediated by meaning, 3–8; reality of being, 3–8, 25–28, 30–33; reality, truth, and belief, 10–12; reality of life, 14–17; intelligibity of reality, 14–17; reality of death, 20–23; love as the ultimate reality, 25–28; reality and the self, 30–33; openness to reality, 14–17; and sacramentality, 47–48; and revelation, 50–54; and myth, 55–57; and the Old Testament, 59–65; and the New Testament, 68–73; and suffering, 75–76; and miracles, 78–81; and the Kingdom of God, 82–83; and the parables, 85–86; and mysticism, 87–90; and theological mysteries, 92–94; and the female, 95–96; and the Archangel Michael, 98–102; and names, 98–102; and the unity of opposites/duality, 107–8; and the personal and universal, 111–13; and matter and spirit, 115–17; and

nature and grace, 118–19; and the natural and supernatural, 121–22; and heaven and earth, 125–26; and time and eternity, 128–29; and knowing and unknowing, 131–33; and consciousness and unconsciousness, 135–37; and humanity and divinity, 138–40; and the cross of Christ, 138–40; and man, 142–44; and God, 145–46; and self-transcending, 148–50; and conclusions, 151–52
reality of being, 3–8, 30–33, 111–17, 131–50
reason, 50–54, 55–57, 92–94
Reign of God. *See* Kingdom of God
relative mystery, 92–94
Relativety, Theory of, 115–17
religious rites, 37–38, 40–41, 68–73, 138–40
resurrection, 14–17, 68–73, 75–76, 78–81, 125–29 138–46, 151–52
revelation, 37–38, 50–54, 59–65, 68–73, 87–90, 92–94, 142–44
Revelation, Book of. *See* Apocalypse of John
rites. *See* religious Rites

sacraments/sacramentality, 47–48, 50–54, 75–76, 87–90, 115–17, 135–37, 138–40
sacredness, 47–48, 59–65, 95–96, 138–40, 148–50
sages, 59–65
salvation/salvation history, 118–19, 128–29, 138–40
Satan, 98–102
Schillebackx, Edward, 75–76
Secret of the Divine Name, 59–65, 125–26
secrets, 37–38, 40–41, 43–45, 59–65, 68–73, 95–96
seeds, 115–17

self, 3–8, 20–23, 25–28, 30–33, 98–102, 111–13, 148–50
self-Actualization. *See* self-Realization
self-communication of God, 50–54, 59–65, 68–73, 87–90, 95–96, 118–22, 145–46
self-consciousness. *See* consciousness
self-realization, 20–23, 25–28, 30–33, 135–37, 138–40, 145–52
self-transcendence, 20–23, 30–33, 111–22, 142–44, 148–50
Semele, 40–45, 145–46, 151–52
Seventh-Day Adventists, 98–102
Shakespeare, William, 3–8
signals of transcendence, 47–48, 50–54, 87–90, 121–22
signs, 78–81, 85–86, 138–40
signs of the times, 50–54, 68–73
silence, 37–38, 50–54, 145–46, 151–52
sin and evil, 30–33, 75–76, 118–19, 138–40
sincerety, 10–12
slavery, 50–54
spirit and matter. *See* matter and spirit and spirituality
spirituality/spiritual experiences, 87–90, 111–13, 121–22, 131–52
Suarez, Fransisco, 3–8
sub-consciousness. *See* consciousness
suffering, 75–76
Summa Theologica of Aquinas. *See* Thomas Aquinas
supernatural, the, 55–57, 78–81, 92–94, 121–22
supernatural existential, 3–8, 121–22
symbol/symbolism, 47–57, 68–73, 78–81, 138–40

Tao, 107–8
temple of God, 151–52
ten commandments, 50–54
theological mysteries, 92–94
theology, 10–12, 145–46
time, 128–29, 138–40

Transcendental Anthropology, 142–44, 148–50
transcendent reality, 10–12, 14–17, 55–57, 68–73, 78–81, 82–83, 87–90, 92–94, 107–22, 135–50
Transcendental Thomism, 3–8
trinity, 37–38, 92–94, 107–8, 115–17, 138–52
truth, 3–8, 10–12, 37–38, 92–94, 131–33

unconsciousness, 135–37, 148–50
unity of opposites, 107–8, 115–17, 138–40
universal and personal, 111–13, 138–40
unknowing, 131–33
unreality, 3–8, 10–12, 14–17, 20–23, 55–57

unveiling, 50–54
Upanishads, 107–8

veils, 50–54
verification of truth, 10–12

Wilde, Oscar, 111–13
wisdom, 14–17, 59–65, 68–73, 95–96, 131–33
Wisdom Books, 59–65
wonders, 78–81
works, 78–81
world, 125–26

Yahweh/I Am Who Am, 59–65, 78–81
Yeshua, 59–65
yin and yang, 107–8

Zeus, 40–41

www.ingramcontent.com/pod-product-compliance
Lightning Source LLC
Chambersburg PA
CBHW022015300426
44117CB00005B/193